Praise for *Loving Cou*

MW01088579

"*Loving Courageously* is one of the best books I have read on the subjects of sex, intimacy, connection and relationships. It is a smart, easy read that is loaded with sage advice and insight from the lens of a highly experienced clinician. *Loving Courageously* is perfect for clients and therapists alike. Every individual and couple will be better off for having read this book. It is practical, interesting, positive and motivating. *Loving Courageously* is my new favorite 'must read book' for my own clients."

-Neil Cannon, Ph.D., LMFT, AASECT Certified Sex Therapist & Supervisor, Denver, Colorado. Instructor, University of Michigan School of Social Work Sexual Health Certificate Program

"My long-time friend and colleague has produced a rare gem—a self-help book that is informative and insightful, yet written in the same conversational, down to earth style one would get if they were sitting in her office. What you read here is what my patients get when they see Barbara—a genuine, caring, intelligent and intensely observant listener who knows what to say–and when to say it! Finally we have a book about how to have a healthier, more satisfying relationship with another person—by learning how to *be* a healthier, more satisfied human being, and how to find a compatible and available partner. I will suggest this book not only to patients, but to everyone I know."

-Philip D. Korenman, M.D.

Psychiatrist, Private Practice, Plano, Texas

"*Loving Courageously: First Me, Then You, Now Us* is a gem! The author Barbara Gold uses relatable stories and metaphors to give the reader critical knowledge and advice for a better relationship with self and partner. She's tackled serious topics like boundaries and compromise in a way that's lively and fun to read. Should be on everyone's 'must read' list."

–Dr. Stephanie Buehler, Psychologist, author of *What Every Mental Health Professional Needs to Know about Sex*

"Barbara Gold has written a user-friendly guide to help you improve your self-esteem. She gently guides the reader to develop the necessary skills in self-care by making one's self first without feeling selfish. Using her wisdom of many decades in the field of psychotherapy along with her numerous references to books she has read, she breaks down the barriers most people find in their way on their journey to self-love. After reading this book you will be well on your way to what she promises—loving yourself courageously!"

–Joe Kort, Ph.D., *LMSW, Certified IMAGO Relationship Therapist, AASECT Certified Sex Therapist & Supervisor of Sex Therapy,* author of *Is My Husband Gay, Straight or Bi?: A Guide for Women Concerned about their Men, Gay Affirmative Therapy for the Straight Cllinician: An Essential Guide,* and others.

LOVING COURAGEOUSLY

First Me, Then You, Now Us

Barbara Gold

Loving Courageously — First Me, Then You, Now Us
Copyright © 2016 by Nugget Press

Published in the United States
ISBN 13: 978-0-692-70886-6

ISBN 10: 0-692-70886-3

Library of Congress Gold, Barbara — Author
227 pages

All names and identifying details of the individuals mentioned in this book have been changed to protect their privacy.

1. Relationship with self 2. self-help 3. relationships 4. sexuality 5. mental health

FIRST EDITON
Cover Design © 2016 Sherry Taylor
Cover Photographer © 2016 Richard Posey

This is a work of non-fiction. All rights remain reserved. Without limiting the rights under copyright reserved above, no part of this publication may be reproduced, stored in or introduced into a retrieval system, or transmitted, in any form, or by any means (electronic, mechanical, photocopying, recording or otherwise) without the prior written permission of Barbara Gold.

To my sons, Geoffrey Gastwirth and Bradley Gastwirth
and my granddaughter, Lily Gastwirth,
who continue to inspire me about love and courage.

Acknowledgements

After spending some fourteen years in a silent tug of war about writing this book, the part of me that wanted to write it finally tugged the hardest and won. Hopefully the long period of indecision culminated in a more knowledgeable version than it would have originally been. It took a village (or, as I like to call it, a 'Think Tank') to write this book. I never could have done it without the help of so many. My gratitude knows no bounds!

Tuesday Thomson, editor and so much more, you have been my rock throughout this process. Not only have you learned to speak in my voice, an amazing feat, you have been my best supporter, cheerleader and hand-holder and steered me back on course when I ran adrift. Donna Mathern, my dear friend--thank you for putting Tuesday and me together! Ellen Leyrer, you have been both an invaluable friend and another pair of editorial 'eyes' when I was too close to the work to see it from a distance. With your excellent editorial skill set, you've taken my references, the final proofing, and the word 'friendship' to a much elevated level. Bridget Boland, you were responsible for creating a coherent conceptualization out of my scattered thoughts about how to organize them, as well as adding your significant editorial prowess to the original manuscript and continued support throughout the process. Brent Meske, you are a never-ending source of patience, encouragement, laughter and comfort, who steered me through the publishing process with skill and your sincere commitment to my satisfaction with the final book—and okay, yes, my 'new best friend!' Richard Posey, my debts of gratitude to you encompass all things Internet, my website, book and website photography and videography, in addition to ad hoc editing, steering me through the perilous world of social media and hand-holding. You'll all definitely be needing a rest! Sherry Taylor, your artistic talent, creativity and tenacity in designing the perfect cover for my book is so deeply appreciated, as is your patience in letting me 'get there.' Jonathan Knopf, my dear cousin, using your impressive journalistic abilities, you were able to take my thoughts and words and weave them into the best possible introduction, as well as catching some of my misses with a keen eye. Niels Skolborg, your willingness to spend time and effort reading and coming up with many suggestions, including my first favorite subtitle was of immense value and very much appreciated. Bobbi Kornblit, author and daughter of my 'adopted' mother, Polly Denur, thank you for your tireless efforts and guidance in the joys and perils of publishing a book. Clarke Newman, my gratitude for your incredible generosity of time and effort, as well as your input on something important I had neglected is tremendous.

To my cousins, Geri Onorato and Susan Knopf, thank you both for marrying into my family and for being such good friends, as well as family, and staunch supporters of my efforts. My brother, Robert Gold, thank you for sharing your 'war stories' from your own books and for your support, encouragement and suggestions. Lloyd Gastwirth, first and foremost, thank you for our two wonderful sons! Your generosity with the book's final proofing with 'fresh eyes' is deeply appreciated.

I owe a debt of gratitude to both my sons, Brad Gastwirth, for your support, encouragement and great suggestions for finding a title for the book, and Geoff Gastwirth, for your excellent input and ideas, and especially for your and Amelia's understanding when my book often precluded me from spending as much time with your precious daughter and my adored granddaughter, Lily, as all of us would have liked!

This book would simply not have been possible without the vast contributions of my clients over the past thirty-five plus years.

You've granted me entry into your places of vulnerability, put your faith and trust in me to hold those sacred, and have taught me at least as much, if not more than I have you. I am humbled by your courage to grow and change, your belief in me and your ability to steer the course on your own for all but forty-five minutes a week, while allowing me the privilege of helping you find which roads you deemed best to travel in that journey. My family, friends and colleagues who read and offered feedback, input and encouragement have been of invaluable support, and I cherish and hold you dear, even as I thank all of you from the bottom of my heart.

About the Author

Barbara Gold is an individual, couples and family therapist, as well as an AASECT certified sex therapist with a private practice in Dallas, Texas. Her book offers new ways of thinking, feeling and being to enhance happiness and life quality.

Believing that loving requires courage, she has written a book drawing on over thirty-five years of psychotherapy practice to help readers discover how to truly love themselves and create healthy relationships. You will learn about things such as boundaries, effective communication, collaborative problem solving and gender differences. You will develop tools to use to create and maintain emotional and sexual intimacy in a committed partnership, as well as learn how to be a "good enough" parent.

Contents

Introduction

Are you able to love and take the best possible care of yourself? Do you feel like a whole, happy person who experiences joy and is truly alive? Overall, do you feel satisfied, grateful and content with your life? Do you believe you have or will find a long-term, healthy and intimate partnership? If the answer to any of these questions is no, you are like many of my clients, and I write this book for you.

From my thirty-five years' experience, I will share with you what works and what doesn't and offer a road map for you to find happiness, heal wounds and become the best possible version of yourself.

Be aware . . . I will challenge some of your beliefs. Despite the many truths in Robert Fulghum's *All I Really Need to Know, I Learned in Kindergarten,* it is also true that by age five we have already taken to heart great amounts of misinformation—some because it was represented as truth and some because our young brains and lack of life experience caused us to interpret things just so. I invite you to question the misinformation that helped form your beliefs, many of which interfere with your ability to achieve happiness and lead a fulfilling life.

I offer an opportunity to discover what you need for healthy emotional self-care to re-write the script you've been handed or developed. You will learn about healthy relationships, including boundaries, effective communication and collaborative problem solving. You will develop a better understanding of gender differences and how to create and maintain emotional and sexual intimacy in a committed partnership. Those of you who have or plan to have children will discover how to be a 'good enough' parent.

My hope is to provide you with new and different ways of thinking, feeling and being, which will enhance your happiness and life quality.

My background and credentials include a master's degree in clinical social work and a two-year postgraduate program in marriage and family therapy. I am trained and certified as a mediator, hypnotherapist, sex therapist, and in collaborative law. I've hosted a radio talk show, *Family Values,* and am licensed as a clinical social worker (LCSW) and marriage and family therapist (LMFT).

The essay format of the book is intended to offer you a more personal experience, as if we are having a conversation in my office. That's how I help best. Perhaps the most important things I hope you take away from this book are the tools to discover your own truths, a much preferable alternative to accepting others'. Read on, if you're open to questioning some of the ideas and beliefs you hold dear. As you do, keep in mind these are *my* thoughts and beliefs.

To quote the master, Carl Rogers, founder of the humanistic psychology movement, "I speak as a person, from a context of personal experience and personal learnings." Take from that what works for you and leave what doesn't. Dim the lights, find the tissues on the table, sit back, relax and welcome to my therapy room!

Preface

Why *Loving Courageously?*

Loving requires courage. It's loving ourselves, which means accepting ourselves, warts and all, just as we do with others we love. It's also taking the risk to let someone become close and important to us, letting them see those warts, and knowing we might suffer hurt or loss. Both are all about courage. Even though it enriches us, loving can hurt. Letting go of old beliefs and behaviors that stand in the way of accepting and loving ourselves is not an easy or painless process, nor is making ourselves vulnerable to others and letting them into our hearts. This book is about relationships—the one we have with ourselves and the ones we have with others. The first, most important relationship we must focus upon is the one with ourselves. Many people miss out on this vitally important ability to develop a healthy sense of self. Our boundaries, which contain our self within them, are in large part what enables us to move in and out between being fully engaged with others back to the reclamation of our whole, independent selves. Once these elements are in place, we move on to look at the other relationships in our lives—some romantic, some not.

We will first look at the relationship to the self and then build upon that to incorporate relationships with others. Along the way, we'll gain a greater understanding of how things evolve, how we begin to form our opinions and beliefs about ourselves, and how our script gets written. We will then explore ways of re-writing the script in order to make it a true and authentic representation of what we believe to be our best self.

Once we have made progress in this ongoing lifelong process, we will be in a better place to look into our relationships with others. It will also help us determine how to find a definition of and means for achieving a healthy intimate partnership without losing ourselves or parts of ourselves. For our purposes, I will be using a heterosexual model for romantic relationships. However, I want to clearly acknowledge the different and often difficult family and social pressures which make this work more challenging for the LGBTQ population. That's not to say it isn't achievable, as I know from professional experience that it very much is. When it comes to couples, I see many of the same dynamics—no matter what the gender. We are all individuals trying to make it work with someone else who is not us. Yet it's surprising how often the expectation they will be just like us is there!

* * *

"One isn't necessarily born with courage, but one is born with potential. Without courage, we cannot practice any other virtues with consistency. We can't be kind, true, merciful, or honest."

–Maya Angelou

Part One

First Me

"To be yourself in a world that is constantly trying to make you something else is the greatest accomplishment."

–Ralph Waldo Emerson

Defining One's Self

Our primary relationship is with ourselves, yet it's the one many people neglect. To develop a healthy sense of self, we must rid ourselves of negative beliefs and messages from the past that we've internalized and learn to put ourselves first. As stated previously, this includes areas such as self-care, boundaries, and having relationships while keeping ourselves intact. If we think of this as being 'centered in self' as opposed to being self-centered, it is both more accurate and has a healthy and positive connotation.

So many of the things we are taught are not necessarily true or beneficial. We learn it is bad to be selfish and good to be selfless. Selfless literally means without a self. I wonder how that can possibly be good. Caring for others is fine, and I guess my chosen profession reflects the value I place on doing so. There is no *one* word in the English language for self-love, as opposed to the often used other two: selfish and selfless. We tend to lose sight of self-love and learn to call it selfish or, heaven forbid, narcissistic. We don't start out that way. Children want what they want, without judgment, until someone introduces them to it. A poignant example was when my then three-year-old granddaughter, seemingly out of the blue, said to me, "I am selfish." Oh, no, I thought, not already. I hastened to tell her that she was *not* selfish, and that wanting something is perfectly fine and doesn't make you selfish, whether or not you get what you want. I wished I could have explained further, but that's about the extent of what a child her age can take in. I repeated the "You are not selfish" part multiple times. I know she didn't hear this from her parents, but already in Mother's Day Out and other peer activities, she was in contact not only with other adults, but with children her own age. Damage control? I sincerely hope so. Someday, when she's old enough to understand, I will tell her, "Feelings are judgment-proof." They just *are*. We're all capable of experiencing the entire range of feelings. Actions and behaviors are very different from feelings. We get to have our feelings, without judgment—whatever they are.

Having shared the absence of one word for self-love with a very wise woman, I learned some delightful news. Unlike English, the French language offers two concepts: *amour-propre,* the love of oneself based on the opinion of others, and *amour-de-soi,* which is self-esteem independent of the opinion of others. Although a French three-year-old won't have read Rousseau's scholarly explanations of these ideas, ideally she'll instead hear her parents, grandparents and friends affirm a healthy self-love. She'll learn to value her own thoughts and opinions, independent of what others think of her. It's my hope that my own granddaughter, as well as my reader can learn the same. And the extra bonus is we don't have to learn to speak French to learn to love ourselves. (Although I'd still love to see someone come up with the *word* in English!)

Writer, teacher and entrepreneur Osi Mizrahi posted an excellent article on *The Huffington Post* entitled, *The Importance of Loving Your Self.* Notice she used two words—your and self. She expanded upon this notion in an earlier post about intimacy. In that article she suggests that

> "people ask themselves if they are a person they would want to be with. If the answer is not yes," she further suggests "asking yourself what changes and improvements could be made by looking at yourself with a loving eye. It is easiest to do this by describing the

kind of people you want to be in relationship with and then implementing those qualities into yourself."

The loving eye is of key importance. More often, people look at themselves through a critical eye. Taking a step back to see oneself with some distance and a lack of negative judgment can yield amazing results.

An example of this might be noticing that your listener has a puzzled or uncomfortable expression on their face and taking the time to wonder what that might be about. You might ask yourself, and them, if you are saying something confusing, or which they might perceive as negative, a boundary violation, or imposing your will upon them. Their answers may yield insight about the content of what you are saying or how you are saying it. Then it is time to clarify, apologize or rephrase depending upon your own perceptions and any feedback you get from them. If there are no verbal or visual cues to notice, you might just take a moment to think about what you are saying and how you are saying it, especially if it constitutes a behavior or attitude of your own you've been working on changing. You then have the opportunity to notice that it's happening again and stop it before it goes any further. For example, if you are working on being less bossy, and you catch yourself being bossy or possibly being perceived that way, you may choose to own it or back up and rephrase.

Mental health professionals know the concept of healthy narcissism, but that seems to be a well-kept secret—a total surprise when I introduce the idea to my clients. Healthy narcissism is not only desirable, it is essential for survival and well-being. Pathological narcissism is a horse of a different color. That's not what I'm talking about.

Rarely are we taught to take care of and give to ourselves, but instead we are encouraged to give to others and put other people's needs before our own. People often label themselves as selfish when they describe doing something for themselves, especially when they've chosen themselves over someone else. Take Sarah, for example. She sits down in my office and says, "My daughter is in fifth grade, and this is the first year I haven't volunteered to be room mother. I feel so guilty and selfish." Let's see, if we include kindergarten, this means Sarah has been her daughter's class room mother for five years, while raising two children and holding down a part-time job. She thinks taking a break from that extra job is a sign of her being selfish. Sadly, this is more typical than not, but certainly *not* true. When we neglect our own needs and wants, there is a vitally important job vacancy. Who, better than yourself, is capable of knowing what you want and need and providing it? The answer, obviously, is no one. Once we pass from childhood to adulthood, there is no one else to fill that role. Many people turn to their spouse or significant other and believe, mistakenly, that their partner can take care of them. Of course we can care for another, but that is different than *taking* care of another. No one other than ourselves can adequately fill that role. When a partner is asked to or attempts to fill this role, all sorts of negative outcomes are very likely to occur.

One very common area where I see this illustrated is around money management. Often one person takes charge of the couple's finances, and to the extent that they are on the same page and able to communicate, this can work out well. Frequently, however, there are missteps. Suzanne took charge of the family finances, and Richard was in agreement with this arrangement. Suzanne was raised to believe that credit card debt was not a problem, so she proceeded accordingly. Richard's family, on the other hand, paid cash for everything, including cars and homes. Relying on Suzanne to manage their money and not sitting down for an in-depth conversation about what that looked like turned into a huge crisis for them—both financially and in their relationship. When Suzanne shared her concern about how large an amount they were paying each month in interest to credit card companies, Richard was shocked and appalled. He had no idea this had been occurring and had gone blissfully about his life, assuming Suzanne had it all under control.

In this instance, Richard blamed Suzanne for creating the debt. Suzanne felt she'd been set up since she had a green light from Richard to do her thing with their money. She had felt burdened by the financial task, but assumed Richard didn't want to be bothered with it. Both parties felt they had been wronged, and many heated arguments ensued. Once the storm passed and clearer heads prevailed, both were able to see their role in creating the unfortunate outcome. Richard expected to be taken care of financially by Suzanne, while she felt responsible for his financial well-being. Both decided that going forward they would jointly manage their money, pay off credit card debt, consult with each other about major purchases, as well as keep abreast of their ongoing financial situation. This is an example of neither Richard nor Suzanne taking care of themselves adequately. They relied upon the other in ways that did not work out well. Had each of them taken better care of themselves and communicated, this would likely have worked out much better for both.

My favorite metaphor for the notion of putting oneself first involves asking the question, "Why, when flying, are we told to put on our oxygen masks first?" With rare exceptions, most will answer that question in the following manner, "Because you can't help someone else if you are unconscious." I'll tell them that is a *true* answer, but it's not the *right* answer. The right answer is that if you lose consciousness, and the cabin pressure isn't stabilized, you will die. Although that might seem obvious, it's still amazing how surprised people are to recognize the truth in that statement. But, we don't think that way. I'm all for helping others, but it is our job to take care of ourselves. If we don't, no one does. Where and how are we taught to love and take the very best care of ourselves? Often, nowhere. And just as often, we're taught not to take care of ourselves lest we be labeled 'selfish.' If self-preservation was intuitive, we wouldn't have to be told to put our masks on first, we'd just do it. After all, no one tells us not to kick out the windows on the plane. Of course, that's so obvious, it needs no mention. How does that 'First Me' instinct become extinguished? As I said earlier, we certainly don't start out that way.

Of course, offering assistance to someone who needs it under any circumstances is a commendable act. No one, including myself, would disagree with that. There are exceptions to 'First Me' of course. For example our children, for whom most of us would take a bullet. Our children need our protection as they are growing up, and putting their needs before our own is often a requirement and a necessity. As our parents age, they may require our care, much as our children did. For every 'rule,' there are always exceptions.

Yet I see many people protecting both their children and their parents unnecessarily and to everyone's detriment. An example is 'failure to launch' (when an adult 'child' stays dependent upon their parents). At its extreme, they may live indefinitely with their parents, enabling destructive behaviors such as lack of financial responsibility, addictions, criminal activity, etc. Another example is allowing ourselves to be hurt in a variety of ways by our parents, such as emotionally supporting a parent at our own expense or permitting disrespectful treatment from a parent. By still trying to be the 'respectful child' and perhaps thereby attempting to protect ourselves from losing our relationship with them, we continue into adulthood a toxic pattern established in childhood.

Evan was the younger of two sons. His mother was never formally diagnosed; however, she showed many signs of mental illness, including paranoia. She held tightly to her sons, never truly permitting them to become individuals who might separate from her emotionally or physically. Evan's older brother was fortunate enough to become involved with a strong woman who was enough of a match for their mother to help him break free, get married, and raise a family. Of course, the conflict between those two women continued throughout Evan's mother's lifetime. Evan went to college and became an accountant. He moved back into his parents' home after finishing graduate school and never left. Although he was successful in his chosen profession and could have financially afforded to leave, he chose not to go. He eventually nursed them both through the illnesses which resulted in their deaths. He remains there still, in his sixties. While he never married or had any long-term intimate relationships, he still says he wants to find the right one. It's extremely unlikely that he will. He was the 'chosen' child once his brother was no longer under his mother's control. Since he never felt as important to her as her first son was, it was gratifying to him to become the chosen son by default. What he gained seemed to him to be sufficient compensation for what he lost.

Self-Talk

One of the ways we can successfully take care of ourselves is by becoming aware of how we talk to ourselves, and whether it's helpful or detrimental to our well-being. I so often hear people speaking about themselves with a total lack of respect, with such contempt and disdain, that I inwardly cringe just hearing them. The voice, which now sounds like their own, did not always. It is other voices, often authority figures, who become internalized by them and now 'belong' to them in a way that feels true and right. They never had the opportunity to examine and choose whether or not that 'voice' speaks *their* truth. Over time, their gut stops protesting, and they settle into a view of themselves and the world that may not really fit them or work for them at all. This is much more common than not.

"I can't believe I was so stupid, am a horrible person, no one could put up with me, would want to be with me, am selfish, weak, thoughtless, fat, unattractive, too needy, bad at relationships..." and a multitude of other put-downs. When it comes to "I'm just feeling sorry for myself, having a pity party," which I frequently hear, they are putting themselves down for what I consider being compassionate for oneself. Why is it when directed toward someone else, we feel compassion, empathy or sympathy? However, when pointed towards ourselves, it somehow becomes something negative, a sign of weakness and self-indulgence.

Mike had been unemployed for nine months. During that time, he had actively pursued all avenues to obtain a job. He had even looked outside his field and been willing to take a large pay cut, but all to no avail. When he described himself as just feeling sorry for himself and that other people have it much worse, I asked him if that's what he would tell his best friend in the same situation. When he said no, of course not, I asked him why he would say this to himself. It saddens but no longer surprises me to bear witness to how cruel to and critical of themselves people can be.

Other ways of putting ourselves (and sometimes others) down include the use of two words I hear often and do not believe in. The first is 'laziness.' I think that's just 'a cover story.' Think of the times you've labeled yourself that way and recall what you were really feeling, as well as checking it out with yourself the next time you use or start to use that word. There are a myriad of possibilities as to what might be happening behind the scenes: anxiety, depression, disinterest, reluctance to do something undesirable, passive aggression, rebellion, and the list goes on. Often I hear people describe themselves (and others) as lazy. If a teen doesn't keep their room clean, there are a number of reasons why not. Some examples are rebellion, wanting to define their space as their own, indifference to clutter, etc. None of these, in my view, constitutes laziness. There's always another explanation or feeling lurking behind that label.

This is another example of negative self-talk and is usually uttered by people who are anything but lazy. It's usually when they aren't being busy, productive, or engaged in a task that they will label themselves this way. My counter to this is: what if you called it relaxing? That's something many people have lost touch with. Having a 'jammies day' when you binge watch a television series you've wanted to see and nothing else gets done seems to me to be a 'mini vacation.' According to the Bible, God rested on the seventh day. If it was a good thing for Him, why do so many of us feel like it is a bad thing? There is an art to relaxation that appears to be turning into a lost one. Many of us seem to neglect relaxation as part of our self-care, and it is an important aspect that needs to be included. Family time doesn't have to mean running from activity to activity. It can just be hanging out at home together doing nothing specific. According to a clergyman I know, the most frequently broken Commandment is resting on the Sabbath. Most people do not adhere to this mandate. If you're not religiously observant, you can pick any day you choose and make it your day of rest. Think self-care, not lazy!

The second word in which I don't believe is 'boredom.' Again, when we say we are bored, something else is going on. Boredom can be a direct outgrowth of so-called 'laziness.' And it often contains or alludes to self-criticism, i.e. there's something I'm not doing right, or I wouldn't be bored. Perhaps we are beset by no good choices of what to do, e.g. chores we'd rather avoid, work we don't want to be bothered with (think tax preparation). It is also a cover for what ails us below the surface. Two of the most common feelings leading to so-called boredom are anxiety and feeling overwhelmed. These may be linked to each other at times. In both instances, we are to some extent immobilized, so any action or activity may require more energy and/or organization than we are able to muster. For lack of a better explanation, we call it boredom. It may also be a manifestation of depression, which is often accompanied by a lack of energy and feelings of fatigue. These are some examples of what may be erroneously labeled as boredom. As a therapist, I'm always curious to know what else is going on when I hear those two words. It might be interesting to ask that question of yourself or others when those labels are applied.

When I hear people speak about themselves with such a negative voice, I always want to say, "Just stop that!" How I wish it were that simple. Simple, it isn't, but do-able, it is. Perhaps the best way to do this is to implement what I call 'the rewind theory of change.' If you are able to identify that you've said something negative to yourself after the fact, you are one step closer to becoming aware. If you are able to notice this happening during the thought, you've taken another step. When you can catch yourself just before you've formed the negative thought, you're 'home.' Keep in mind that this change process will be back and forth, not steadily progressive, as that's the way change works across the board.

Having defined the problem, let's look at some things that can help us resolve it. In addition to acquiring the necessary skills to take proper care of ourselves, we will benefit from utilizing whatever reasonable resources are available to us. Most women will have a friend to offer them support, 'a shoulder to cry on.' Although this is true for some men, it is less likely to be the case. Most men don't turn to other men for emotional support. They are more likely to either ask for it from their significant other or the women in their lives. Depending on the dynamics, family can be a great source of support, as well, for both genders. There are organizations for both men and women that also provide support—some formal, some not. The ManKind Project, is a group in which men are able to be their authentic selves and garner support from other men. There are many groups for both men and women around specific issues such as Alcoholics Anonymous, Al Anon (for people in relationships with alcoholics or people who are chemically dependent), grief, abuse, divorce, depression, etc. There are also Meetup groups with a wide variety of themes. Finding groups isn't difficult; however, sharing and being vulnerable in such a setting requires courage.

I believe strongly in the benefits of exercise. Although I've merely dabbled in yoga, I've yet to meet a practitioner who didn't sing its praises. Meditation, journaling, and other activities that help you center yourself and reduce life's stresses are all well worth pursuing. Healthy eating and maintaining physical health are vital aspects of taking care of oneself. The healthier we are, the better we feel. Feeling capable of financially supporting and taking care of ourselves helps build self-esteem, and giving to others (in the proper order!) also contributes to our sense of well-being. If you think about it, all these are aimed at taking good care of your 'self,' whether it's on your own or with the help and support of others.

Just in case this book isn't enough, let's take a peek into what happens in therapy. It probably goes without saying that I'm a believer in the power and benefits of therapy. I do suggest that people consider speaking with, or even meeting with, more than one therapist before embarking upon that process. It is so important that people feel they are talking to someone who is competent to help them and whom they can trust. The fit between client and therapist is very important. As the client, you are a consumer of a service, and therefore entitled to get the service that best suits you. Because therapists are often seen as authority figures, many clients fail to speak up when they are dissatisfied or want something to change in the therapeutic process. I strongly encourage people to tell their therapists if something isn't working for them. Aside from the greater benefits they can derive from therapy as a result, it is an opportunity to practice taking care of themselves in relationships (in this case their relationship with their therapist), thereby developing a skill in an environment, that is ideally suited to be the safest place to do so.

In addition to having the right to make the choice of therapist, you have the absolute right not to be negatively judged by anyone. If you think that is occurring, I urge you to ask. If you aren't satisfied with the answer or if it happens again, it may be time to make a change. Therapy must be a safe place, whether you're working alone or with a partner. It is the place where you can be your most vulnerable self. You can acknowledge your flaws and any shame you may carry only to discover that the therapist continues to accept you without any negative judgment or rejection. That is an invaluable validation of your worth. I don't think there's anything that could shock me at this point. If someone proved me wrong, that still wouldn't constitute a negative judgment. I believe this is true for more therapists than not; however, there are some who do better work than others.

Tissue boxes, strategically placed around the room, are an essential staple for any therapist. Someone once suggested that I should hang a sign on my door entitled 'The Crying Room,' as many tears are shed inside those walls. Unfortunately, many people equate crying with weakness. Although males are acculturated not to cry, this inhibition also applies to many women. Clearly, when people are crying they are feeling pain, and most of us do not enjoy feeling pain. I encourage clients to cry. It is a way of releasing and potentially letting go of the pain. Unshed tears go hand-in-hand with suppressed feelings, which are likely to manifest in unhealthy ways, whether emotional, physical or both.

Many people believe that being in therapy or taking medication for depression, anxiety or other emotional distress is also a sign of weakness. I counter that belief with my own. I believe that it takes a great deal of courage to go to therapy, to express and feel pain, to endeavor to change and grow without labeling oneself negatively. When someone chooses to enter therapy, it is most often because they are in emotional pain. Too often we judge ourselves negatively for our emotional pain or our inability to overcome it by ourselves. I often use the example of diabetes and ask people if they would judge others or themselves if they required insulin to repair a deficit in their body's functioning. Of course, the answer is no. We do not understand enough at this time how much our physiology plays a role in our psychological well-being. Depression and anxiety, to the extent that they constitute a clinical diagnosis, are not feeling states that people can 'snap out of.' Unfortunately, people who have not experienced severe depression and anxiety may fail to understand this fact. Severe depression can lead to suicidal thoughts, plans and actions. Severe anxiety may immobilize a person to the point that they are avoiding necessary functions. As far as we have come toward understanding emotional problems as a normal part of life, many of us still cling to the belief that we should be able to solve all of our own problems. I liken psychotherapy to visits with physicians when we experience physical ailments or ill health. Just as there is no judgment when our bodies need care, I hope we can reach the point where there is no judgment when our emotions need care, as well.

These are some of the many things we learn incorrectly or fail to learn, which interfere with our happiness and our ability to form and maintain healthy relationships in our adult lives. The three things that are the most difficult to do are loving and caring for ourselves, being in a healthy committed relationship, and raising children. I find it more than unfortunate that none of these vitally important things is taught to us. We learn from example, often we learn what *not* to do, as opposed to what to do, from whatever sources are available to us. For the most part, we are thrown into the deep end of the pool without having had any lessons, and simply told to *swim*. No small surprise that many people find themselves floundering.

● ● ●

Who Teaches Us?

As I mentioned earlier, at a young age we often internalize and adopt the beliefs of external authority figures, using those beliefs as the guide by which we live our lives. Below we'll examine who and what influences us as we grow.

Parents

Our first teachers are our parents or parenting figures. Our entire family of origin, including siblings, also plays a significant role in our first life lessons, as well as subsequent lessons learned as we are growing up. As a parent myself, I am very aware of the fear parents have of being judged and found wanting. No one is perfect. We can't parent perfectly, either. Nonetheless, with rare exceptions, most of us do the very best we can rearing our children. I urge you to consider a concept I will introduce below in terms of being a 'good enough' parent. Sometimes our best falls short of the mark, and our children suffer the consequences. The transgenerational nature of parenting makes it easier to continue destructive patterns, if we do not recognize and correct them. Children learn what they live.

When my children were young, I came across the concept referred to by British pediatrician and psychoanalyst, Donald Winnicott as the "Good Enough Mother."

A study was done in which the mothers interacted and the toddlers ran off to do what toddlers do, from time to time checking back in with mom and then running off again. At the end of this study, the conclusion was that all a child needs is a 'Good

Enough' mother. This holds true for fathers, as well. I can't tell you what a relief it was to hear that being good enough was truly good *enough*! The entire realm of human roles and behavior can easily be encompassed into this 'good enough' category. For those who set their bar impossibly high, it can bring a huge sigh of relief. Let me be clear that I'm not advocating mediocrity—a suspicion which I know occurs to many of my clients. I just firmly believe that we do our very best even if that best is better at some times than others. The argument I usually get from people is that they could have done more. I counter with, "If you could have, you would have."

A well-meaning parent, who wants to encourage their child to succeed academically, does not intend damage when he or she says, "Four A's and a B. Why not five A's?" I have heard various versions of this so many times over the years. What message is sent to the child? You get no credit for what you *did* achieve, merely a criticism for what you did not, and, as a result, the message that the child receives is that if you're not perfect, you're not good enough. The quest for perfection begins here and continues into adulthood. In addition, the implication that perfection is possible, or even desirable, becomes reinforced. This is only one of many such examples of how well-meaning parents may negatively impact their child's sense of self and self-esteem without intending to so. This is a time when I generally make the comment that the one outcome guaranteed every time in the pursuit of perfection is failure.

Jeff exemplifies this perfectionism very clearly. Although he is a physician, well-respected in his area of specialization by his peers and patients alike, he is always second guessing himself. When I asked him if he had any ideas about when this consistent feeling of not being good enough began, he told me about his parents. Both were college professors who placed great emphasis upon education and achievement. They believed that complacency was the enemy and made certain that Jeff never came close to achieving that comfort level. Whatever his achievements, his parents would scrutinize them so thoroughly that he would be left with the distinct impression that whatever he did wasn't quite good enough. He was often compared to his peers and felt his parents had a higher opinion of them than of him. It took him a long time to trust and believe that he was actually doing a very good job in his work and his life. This entailed understanding that his parents spent their lives trying to be better in order to please their parents at the urging of their own families. That this theme continued through yet another generation is not at all surprising. Once Jeff understood the transgenerational dynamics, he was better able to loosen the stranglehold this had been for him his entire life.

How do parents determine what is true about their children? Since they are biased and unable to be objective, their 'truth' is the story they tell themselves and others about their kids. These stories are based upon the parents' own perceptions of truth, then handed down to their children as fact. Parents see their children through many filters. One filter is their own beliefs and knowledge about people. Another filter is their worry that something bad will happen to their child. A third is often the fear that they will not be a good enough parent, ill-equipped as they feel for the job—especially with a first child.

Most, if not all of us, are familiar with the idea that we do not want to be like our parents in some ways. We can become so immersed in this that it actually causes us to choose an extreme opposite behavior or point of view, and this isn't necessarily the best option either, e.g., "My parents were too strict, so I set few, if any, limits for my children."

Sometimes linked to this is a very significant filter—projection of the parent's own issues onto their child. What we may not be aware of is that we are projecting onto our child aspects or characteristics we possess that the child may not possess themselves. This projection, which occurs in many relationships, may be a conscious recognition of a similar trait or behavior, or may be totally unconscious. For example, a parent who remembers the pain of being the last one chosen for sports teams may be so fearful of this happening to their child that it is indirectly communicated and impacts the child's confidence about their ability. Kids pick up adult vibes, even when parents believe otherwise. Those vibes, along with words uttered repeatedly and often enough, may unwittingly create reality for the child. Expectations are often linked to outcome. If I expect you to fail— and consistently put that message out to you—then you may, indeed, stop succeeding. Those who project may or may not recognize the source of this behavior. The parent who holds grudges, but cannot see that in themselves, may project that onto the child. They may then accuse their child of doing something that the child may not actually be doing, or has emulated from their parent's example. The expression, "You spot it; you got it" sums it up well.

Children are receptacles for all sorts of information from parents: some of it accurate, some of it not. Most importantly, young children see parents as the arbiters of truth. As one therapist I know put it, "Parents are those giant people on a movie screen— much, much larger than life." Maybe that's why it's often such a blow when kids become older and actually figure out our true size!

Almost every time Leslie referenced herself, her mother would chastise her by saying "I–I–I, all you ever talk about is yourself." I wondered who else she should have been invested in talking about. She, like myself, was brought up in the era of 'Children should be seen and not heard.' Statements like the one Leslie's mother made and the silence imposed upon children left them with the clear idea that being self-focused was a bad, and yes, *selfish* thing. This thinking helps erode a sense of self and teaches one to focus instead on others. Yet, like Leslie, we are often able to remain alive and well, albeit stifled. Taken to the extreme, one's self is lost in the process. As a result, we may create a 'pseudo self' or 'false self.' This is the persona we present to the world, but it is not our authentic self. This comes about when we feel we must hide who we truly are in order to be accepted and loved. When we adopt this pseudo self, it is at the sacrifice of the authentic self. That is too high a price to pay. We lose our ability to be our natural self and to approach others in a truly open and vulnerable way. Although we feel more protected by not showing that openness and vulnerability, we lose in terms of our freedom to be ourselves, as well as our ability to feel a deep connection with others.

There was good reason for the popularity of Al Franken's Stuart Smalley character on *Saturday Night Live.* His words and the subsequent book, *I'm Good Enough, I'm Smart Enough, and Doggone It, People Like Me*, resonated with many, as did the broader concept of daily affirmations.

Many times I'm asked by clients if I get tired of hearing the same things and responding in the same ways. My answer is always "no." I understand and value the need for this repetition in the process of growth and change. The movie *The Help* (based on the book by Kathryn Stockett) illustrated an adult parental caregiver who understood the need for the child to hear the positives many times to overcome all the negative messages she'd already received about herself in order to develop a healthy sense of herself and her value. This caregiver character was truly a perceptive as well as loving woman who understood the need for many repetitions to instill these positive messages that the child was intelligent, a good person and had value. I've heard it said that it can take seven positive messages to undo one negative message. I believe it.

One of my favorite sayings is that "we teach people how to treat us." If we don't feel that we deserve to be treated well, that's the message we send to others. If, on the other hand, we love and respect ourselves and expect others to do the same, then that's a very different message. For those who don't, loving oneself doesn't come easily or quickly to people, but with enough courage, time, work and repetition we can get there. It is so worth the effort!

Family Roles and Rules

Birth order and family roles play an important part in how we develop, and there are many different ways in which this manifests itself. Are there so many children that most feel lost in the shuffle? Do we learn to 'be in charge' like little adults because we're the oldest? Are we the 'baby' who 'gets away with murder?'

(Just ask any oldest child.) How does our birth order impact our personalities, sense of self, leadership qualities, or sense of responsibility? We often hear people describe themselves as the older, younger or middle child. There is an assumption that certain attributes apply to each. Generally, the oldest tends to take more of a leadership role and is inclined to take charge. Again generally, the youngest may be more passive and more likely to expect others to take care of them or have a more passive personality. The middle child is often referred to as the 'forgotten child' and may react by receding into the background, by acting out negative behaviors or overachieving to gain attention. It is not uncommon for people to perpetuate these stereotypes into adulthood. These are generalizations and certainly don't apply to all children or families.

Other aspects of roles, not necessarily dependent on birth order, exist. We might be 'the angel child,' striving for perfection, and avoiding blame and disapproval at almost any cost. Or perhaps we are the 'devil child,' rebellious, breaking rules, and receiving negative attention. Our roles come in many shapes and sizes. We might be a 'parentified child,' the confidante of one or both of our parents. This child is expected to be an adult to whom the parent can turn for comfort in an unfortunate reversal of roles. They are treated as a partner who replaces the spouse, and are generally thrown into a multitude of adult roles well before the child is equipped to play those roles. This dynamic is common, unfortunately, for although it gives a sense of power and importance to the child, it simultaneously robs them of the freedom to truly *be* a child, unsaddled by adult responsibilities. It is ultimately unhealthy for both the child and the entire family. Being the 'chosen child,' perks notwithstanding, not only burdens a child, but may continue into adulthood, and in extreme cases, the adult child remains in the position of caregiver to the parent (or parents) to such an extent that they never 'leave home'— either literally and/or figuratively. This is the most destructive version of the expression 'failure to launch.'

Almost every family has its rules. Things such as, "Don't jump on the furniture" and "Eat your vegetables" are some examples, along with everything else the parents deem important to teach their children. These rules include the 'do's and don'ts' of behavior, and oftentimes feelings and their expression, as well. These rules are a necessary part of civilizing kids, as well as preparing them to go out into the world and fare well. Limits are so important for us all, but especially in the case of children who are learning how to behave with others, as well as on their own. A child with no limits again exemplifies the metaphor of being thrown into the deep end of the pool without knowing how to swim. It may look like they're having it their way, but underneath is a great deal of fear and uncertainty. As a therapist I knew put it, "Kids need to know there is someone there to keep them from killing themselves." He was referring to adolescents, but the concept of danger applies to children of all ages. For some parents, setting limits is not difficult. For others, this isn't the case. Once again, we look to how we were raised. If the limits were moderate, extreme or missing, we try to do better with our own kids When we have and implement a reasonable set of rules for our children, it's very uncomfortable to encounter other children who don't seem to have any rules at all.

Too often our socialization and the simultaneous teachings encourage us to strive for perfection. As I said before (and may again), one thing we can be certain of is that if we try to be perfect, we will always fail. Believing and fully accepting this is a huge relief. Our beliefs inform our thoughts, our thoughts inform our feelings, and our feelings inform our behavior. Keeping that in mind, we can begin to realize just how important our beliefs are to our sense of well-being. If I believe the world is populated by people who are mostly trustworthy, I will act from that place toward my fellow man. Conversely, if I believe the world is populated by people who are untrustworthy, I will expect the worst from people. The bottom line here is how we feel within ourselves and about ourselves. We can change our beliefs. We can change our behavior. We can also change our emotions. Knowing that they are tied together is very important. It helps us become more organized and empowered.

Related closely to limits are boundaries. These two words are often used interchangeably, so I'd like to clarify the difference. Boundaries belong to each of us. We have boundaries around our bodies, our need for space, our need to be treated respectfully, our willingness to act in certain ways, etc. When someone crosses our boundaries, we are best served when we set limits with them about what is and what is not acceptable to us. To the degree that we are able to maintain our boundaries and protect ourselves and others using those boundaries, we will feel good about ourselves and be received well by others. If our boundaries are too permeable, we will feel repeatedly hurt and invaded. If they are impenetrable, we will keep everyone at arm's length. As in all things, there is a middle ground, a healthy balance, which we are all capable of creating.

Young children are limited in their ability to maintain boundaries; however, they can be quite creative in their own ways. My son was mindful of and showed respect to his then three-year-old (she's four now!) daughter's boundaries. He has learned that if he tells her that something is going to occur ahead of time (e.g. picking up toys, taking a bath), she responds much better when the time comes to put the plan into action. He respects her need (boundary) for some warning to get her ready to move from one activity to another. I suspect she had something to do with teaching him this by resorting to some sort of behavior or behaviors he didn't want to see, until he caught on. Guess they make a pretty good team! If she balks or refuses, he will then need to set a limit on her behavior and quite likely give a consequence (time out, etc.). Hopefully this helps clarify the difference between boundaries and limits. I think it is always preferable to refer to consequences (or natural consequences) with children, as opposed to 'punishment.' Life will continually reinforce natural consequences, so this is laying the groundwork for expectations. The notion of parents punishing their children does not feel good to the children, and most often doesn't feel good to the parent, either. It's not a crime and punishment scenario, merely a natural consequence of behaviors.

Teachers

Teachers impact our lives almost as much as parents, both positively and negatively. Receiving praise from a teacher can go a long way toward instilling a sense of competence and pride in a child. When a child does well and is provided with positive feedback from their teachers, it can greatly increase their self-esteem and confidence. Warren had very little confidence in his academic abilities. A large part of this was the fact that he had not yet been diagnosed with Attention Deficit Disorder and dyslexia, which greatly interfered with his ability to learn. His teacher in second grade recognized his exceptional ability in math and encouraged him to progress beyond what his fellow classmates were doing. Not only did Warren develop an avid interest in math, he also was able to experience himself as succeeding academically for the first time. After he was diagnosed properly and given appropriate assistance in supporting his learning differences, his other areas of academic performance improved as well.

I greatly admire teachers. As a former teacher, I know just how hard a job it is, and I am so often inspired by the level of dedication and care so many bring to the task. Warren's teacher began a process that enabled him to feel better about himself, stop the negative messages about his academic performance and provided him an area in which to begin to excel.

Unfortunately, not all teachers have a positive impact. Negative experiences leave their mark as well—at times indelibly. Susan was deeply imprinted by her third grade teacher of whom she has vivid memories some fifty years later. This teacher would routinely verbally and emotionally abuse the eight-year-olds in her class by ridiculing them in front of their peers and abusing her power to the degree that one child was so afraid to ask permission to go to the restroom that she actually wet herself in front of the class. Susan's identification with this girl, and empathy for her feelings of humiliation, remain a part of her still. The damage done to thirty or so children a year, for at least several decades, is inestimable. Of course, we're talking ancient history here. The world has changed in ways unimaginable to Susan or to any of us who suffered at the hands of cruel and unkind teachers. These days, parents are far more involved. I applaud the growth in understanding and knowledge of both educators and parents, as well as the involvement and generally 'being there,' which many of the parents today exemplify.

Religious Teachers

Religion and its concomitant teachings may be a powerful source of imprinting. Religious teachings can be positive and beneficial. How civilized would our world be without the Ten Commandments or their equivalent? What follows next is my opinion, and it is yours to consider or reject, as are all my ideas and opinions on this and any subject. Religion can become a problem when beliefs and teachings portray a world of black-and-white, where the good guys (us) wear white hats, and the bad guys (everyone who believes differently or falls short of the tenets and rules of our faith) wear black ones. The rules can create a useful structure, but can also create such a strict and punitive superego (our own personal judge, if you will) to the point that we can't contemplate a different reality at all without suffering greatly. To do so might create a dissonance so great it renders us full of self-loathing and misery. This may be strongly akin to brainwashing and difficult to overcome; however, it can be done. This is true for any and all religions when the extremes distort reality for the believers to a point where reason departs and independent thoughts and beliefs are vanquished. Over time, we've had numerous examples of this extremism. A recent example is that of suicide bombers. Unfortunately, however, there is plenty of room for damage short of the extremes.

Peers

When we are very young, we begin to interact with those around our own age. As toddlers, we begin with what is known as 'parallel play.' Despite the separateness of activities, there is a sense of togetherness that begins there. As we grow older and become more aware of ways of interacting, we begin the process of playing together. This experience teaches us plenty of facts and information. Robert Fulghum says we learn to share our toys, not to hit, etc. These are important life lessons, of course, and as Fulghum says, they come up over and over again in life in more adult forms. How our peers receive and react to us helps us define ourselves. If we feel generally liked and accepted, we tend to like ourselves. If we feel bullied, ostracized, or humiliated, then we tend to feel bad about ourselves. We hope to figure it out so we can fix it and our peers will then accept us. Or, we tell ourselves we're better than them, and that's why they treat us badly. We never really believe that deep down; we *know* it must be us. For children, the world is small and revolves around them. This isn't surprising given their short life span and limited exposure to the world. As sweet, kind and loving as children can be, they can also be brutal, hurtful and hateful. As children, we begin with knowing nothing except our needs and wants, and we have to be taught to fit into the civilized world.

Once peers become a real source of learning, they also become very important. Close friendships begin to develop, as do groups or cliques. As childhood progresses, this becomes more defined and sophisticated. A sense of belonging is usually desirable, and if not experienced, results in feelings of social isolation. When Danielle was in middle school, she was befriended by Julie. Danielle was in the 'popular' crowd—the cool kids. Julie was a newcomer to the school who possessed many positive qualities. Danielle felt flattered that Julie sought her out and wanted to make friends with her. Julie fit right in with Danielle's group of friends and for a time, things went very well. It wasn't until Danielle became aware that Julie was becoming divisive between herself and some of the other girls, that Danielle began to feel mistrust for Julie. As things unfolded and Julie became less interested in a friendship with Danielle, it seemed apparent to

Danielle that she had been used for a purpose—to gain entry into the cool crowd. Once there, her usefulness to Julie ceased to be of importance. This was deeply wounding to Danielle, who had been fooled by Julie and was hurt by her behavior. When she shared this story, I suggested to her that she was not, as she told me, a fool. I told her that anyone can fool us if they really want to, no matter how intelligent we may be. If we are fooled, this does not make us a fool. The responsibility lies with the party who deceives us. This was an important lesson learned for Danielle.

It's very often the case that as children and especially as adolescents, the choices made in friends will mirror our experience in our family of origin. We seek out what feels familiar and comfortable, although not necessarily what is good for us. In Danielle's case, her mother was very warm and loving, but also very manipulative. Over time, she learned that she couldn't trust her mother. This was a very difficult and painful lesson, but one she needed to learn. At the time she befriended Julie, Danielle did not yet have this awareness, so she was drawn in, as we all are, by what she knew from experience. Unfortunately, this may well continue into adulthood. As we grow and gain greater understanding about our families, the people we encounter, and insight about ourselves, our choices have an opportunity to change along with us and to become healthier ones, no matter what our age.

Other Sources of Impact

Our Own Perceptions

Childhood trauma and events help shape us. Children are bound by their perceptions. When I was somewhere around three years old, my parents left me alone in our apartment and went outside to visit with our neighbors. Since she was close by, my mother was confident that she would hear me if I called her. I cried hysterically for what seemed like hours upon awakening and finding myself all alone. I was afraid to get out of bed, feeling like I was totally alone in the world. When my mother finally came in to check on me, she discovered me in this completely distraught state. My sense of abandonment was profound. The memory is etched clearly to this day, sixty plus years later. Did my mother really abandon me? Of course not. Was my experience of being abandoned real? Absolutely.

Of course, there are actual instances of trauma for many children. These may include emotional, verbal, physical abuse, sexual molestation or neglect. Those are the abuses most difficult to heal, and which, understandably, most adults prefer to avoid dealing with due to the deep level of pain. It is never welcome news when I tell people that the only way I know to heal these wounds is to go through the experience. I know of no way around, under or over to get to the other side. The other side is, of course, healing. In my practice I have encountered stories of abuse so great that they defy all reason and rationality, many at the hands of mentally ill adults. The damage is extreme and difficult to hear, no matter how many times a therapist has heard it, let alone for the person to live through and revisit once again in therapy. These occurrences are often the most dramatic examples of what can happen transgenerationally, when healing does not occur.

Much more can be said on the subject, but for now I want to clarify types of abuse. Sometimes emotional abuse is not verbal, but verbal abuse is *always* emotional abuse, as is physical abuse. What I mean by this is that a parent or other adult can behave in ways that are extremely hurtful to a child without saying a word. A good example of this is refusing to speak to a child or totally ignoring them. Physical abuse needs clarification and often is in the eye of the beholder. To many parents, spanking is not abusive. To others it is. To children, being grabbed by the arm may be experienced as abusive, even if the parent's intent was to protect them from potential harm. The last speaks again to a child's perception. However, there are instances of physical abuse, which no one would deny as abusive—beatings, breaking bones, burning, hair pulling—in short, deliberately inflicting pain, and this may encompass outright torture. What I often hear from adults is that they do not consider themselves to have been abused by parents who so clearly (to me) were abusive. This is attributable in part to the facts that it was 'business as usual' as well as a natural inclination to protect one's parents. Given a choice, abused children will almost always return to the abusive parent when presented with another alternative. This is often shocking to other people, but it makes sense in terms of who they love and what they are familiar with. As adults, it's never a pleasant discovery to learn that one has been victimized—especially by people who were supposed to love and protect us.

The Courage to Heal by Ellen Bass and Laura Davis opened the door to speaking out about child sexual abuse. Although their original book dealt only with females, the subsequent growth in awareness about male sexual abuse has broadened understanding and information, most recently in the film *Spotlight*. Additionally, when the perpetrator is a family member, it greatly increases both the complexity and the difficulty in healing, or, as in the case of *Spotlight*, when the perpetrator is a trusted priest—almost the embodiment of God. In my opinion, it is not necessary to forgive the abuser, as many believe; forgiveness is something earned, and is more for the person who caused injury than the injured person. Acceptance, letting go of the negative feelings, and moving on can be achieved with or without forgiveness. Sometimes the abuser is no longer alive, is not known or has not asked for forgiveness or even acknowledged that the abuse occurred. Although forgiveness is an option, it is not a necessity.

In my experience there has never been an exception to the rule that abused children blame themselves for the abuse and carry the shame, which rightfully belongs to the abusers. This shame manifests itself in many different ways. Some people totally repress the abuse and have no memory of it occurring. At some point the memory may return as the unconscious gradually presents the person with clues and cues that trigger feelings. Over time this may become much like pieces of a puzzle, which eventually begin to assemble themselves into a whole picture, and the memory resurfaces. Sometimes this part of the process is a very slow one, and people are both anxious and afraid to know what they have not yet remembered. This can be especially painful and create a great deal of anxiety and often depression. The reason these 'victims' are called 'survivors' is both because it feels much better than being a victim and because there are many who do not, in fact, survive. It is almost essential that psychotherapy becomes a part of this process if healing is to occur.

Healing the shame is the most crucial focus for sexual abuse survivors. The weight of this burden affects their lives in a multitude of ways. It negatively impacts their self-esteem, their ability to trust and be open with other people, and inevitably, their sexuality. Clearly, this also impacts their relationships with others.

Interestingly, though not surprising, most people's first memory of childhood is centered on something they experience as traumatic. This may include injuries, surgeries, death, witnessing something violent, or merely a perception of something more innocuous, which seemed dangerous or felt emotionally impactful. Even though this is not true for everyone, it is common. For some, however, the first memory is a happy one.

In John Irving's *The World According to Garp*, Garp's young son hears the word 'undertow,' a word with which he's unfamiliar, as 'under toad', and his imagination runs wild in a terrifying way. He believes there is a giant toad monster in the bottom of the ocean he must elude, since he's heard the warning about being careful of the undertow. On a lighter note, some of the misperceptions of children can be both extremely funny and charming. Many years ago, there was a television show entitled *Kids Say the Darndest Things*. I would submit that kids also *hear* the 'darndest' things. As children, just like Garp's son, we see the world as it appears to us. Seldom can we, as adults, look back with a broad enough view to understand how our thinking processes as a child evolved into adult thoughts. It seems like somehow they just did. There may have been serious and uncorrected perceptions much like those of the under toad, only far more detrimental to our well-being.

From time to time someone will walk into my office stating that they had a wonderful childhood and great parents. I'm not denying the possibility of this; however, no childhood nor parent is perfect. This declaration is usually an invisible sign held up to me stating, "Don't go there." Our instinct to protect our parents is a part of this, but at least an equal or greater part is our need to protect ourselves from possibly painful truths. Greg always thought of himself as an independent child, and in the process of exploring the reasons for this, he came to understand that he was independent because he had to be, as a result of a great deal of parental neglect. Since children are egocentric, they will always blame themselves. For Greg, it was no different. When his mother wouldn't come to his rescue, he took this to mean that he was bad for having his needs. He just had to be a better boy so Mom would love him enough to give him the care that he needed, and so he wouldn't be a bother to her. In the meantime, he learned to be extremely self-sufficient and received a great deal of positive reinforcement for it. It wasn't until many years later in therapy that he was able to face these truths. Greg was certainly not the only one to enter my office with the perfect childhood announcement and exit with a very different understanding about himself and his parents.

There are many reasons why a parent might neglect a child, and they range from not having another alternative to what constitutes abuse. Working to support a family without adequate childcare, depression, illness, mental illness and having too many kids are just some of the many reasons. There is a continuum regarding neglect. Recently there was a news story about a two-year-old boy left in his crib with a space heater for over twenty-four hours who died of hyperthermia. His parents were using and making drugs at the time, and never checked on him or responded to his cries for help. This is a starkly brutal example of neglect resulting in the ultimate extreme of abuse—death. I am not entirely on board with the fact that neglect is used as a separate category from abuse, as it tends to negate and soften the reality that neglect can often be a form of abuse.

When children encounter situations that engender emotional responses in them, they must learn how to understand and deal with their feelings. Just like the experiences of adults, children's experiences are replete with opportunities for an emotional response. How the child reacts to their own feelings, as well as how others react to the child's feelings plays an important role in shaping both the feelings themselves and the child's response to those feelings.

Inner Children

Ego Psychology offers a very useful take on the different internal parts of ourselves. I'm not talking about multiple personalities (e.g. *Sybil*) when I say we all have inner child parts. We may be conscious of them or not.

The term 'inner child' is often used; however, it's worth defining for our purposes. Whatever our chronological age, at a fairly early time we have internalized earlier versions of ourselves. We may be ten or forty years old chronologically, but within us remain earlier selves. These versions may play a small or large part in our lives, about which we may be unaware. At any given time, these internalized parts, which co-exist simultaneously, may interact with each other as well as with our current self. It can be a cooperative or competitive interaction or both. For example, I am especially aware of my four-year-old and fifteen-year-old selves. The four-year-old is easily wounded and can go to a terrible place of shame with a profound sense of both worthlessness and helplessness. Fortunately, she's rarely making guest appearances these days. It took me many years and a lot of work to convince her to sit back and let the adult me handle things. Now that she doesn't dissolve into that painfully helpless place, it's much easier to find her endearing. I feel almost as protective of her as I do my real life children.

My other easily recognizable younger self is my adolescent. My fifteen-year-old is actually fun! She just wants to enjoy herself and have a good time. All she needs from me is some balance between playtime and responsibility. She's got her place in my life, but doesn't run it. I give her plenty of time to run loose, to be free and joyful.

That's my own example of how inner children manifest themselves. One of my biggest hopes for others is that they can embrace all parts of themselves, even the parts they don't particularly like, and love themselves without reservation and wholeheartedly. To that end, most people are much more tolerant of others' flaws than their own. I often suggest to clients that they look at another person (or a child the same age as their inner one) to see if they would have the same negative judgment, or if they would feel compassion instead of contempt or disdain. The obvious answer is no negative judgment for another.

Too often, people dislike and have strong negative feelings about their inner children. It is reflected in their self-talk, which I referenced earlier. In order to truly love ourselves, we must find a way to embrace ourselves entirely, including the parts we don't particularly like. Ironically, we accept the flaws of others we love, yet when it comes to ourselves, it's a much more difficult task. This brings to mind the concept of 'The Shadow Self' developed by Carl Jung, a highly esteemed Swiss psychiatrist, whose research was deeply rooted in psychoanalysis. But Jung eventually disagreed with many of Freud's theories and developed his own. Our shadow (darker side) follows us wherever we go. Unlike Peter Pan, we just can't be separated from it. It's our challenge to accept it, to change what we desire and to love ourselves including our shadow. For us to know we deserve 'the whole loaf,' and that wanting it is a good thing, is essential. In addition, and of utmost importance, we need to know without a doubt that if we have failed to learn that we are lovable and deserving as children, it does not mean there is something wrong with us or that it was our fault.

Feelings

Feelings are a very important part of each of us; yet, it can be difficult to learn how to manage them in a healthy manner. One of the most difficult feelings for both children and adults is anger. Unfortunately, we are most often not taught how to express our own anger so it's no surprise that we don't know how to teach our children how to express theirs appropriately. Perhaps it's okay to slam the door to your bedroom, but not okay to tell someone you hate them. If things aren't spelled out clearly, so a child knows what is permissible, the child is often left with a global sense that anger is bad and with no way in which to safely discharge it.

Whether intentional or not, our families, friends and society teach us about expressing emotions. Stereotypically, men have been allowed to express only one emotion—anger—while women have been strongly discouraged to express any anger at all. The inability to deal effectively with anger leads us into trouble in the area of resolving conflict. "Don't be angry or you will be punished." is more commonly heard than, "It's fine for you to be angry and to express it in an acceptable way."

I can't overemphasize the importance of such a deficit in learning. It spills over into our lives as adults and into our relationships. Road rage, the inability to manage anger, and physical abuse are some of the unfortunate outcomes of this significant omission. For males especially, anger is used to cover more vulnerable feelings such as hurt, sadness, fear and helplessness. Of course, females may manifest this as well; however, our culture has historically allowed a greater range of expression of feelings for women than it has for men. I'm pleased to see this changing, but it's not changing as quickly as I'd like!

So let's address what has changed. Many years ago, Harriet Goldhor Lerner wrote a wonderful book entitled, *The Dance of Anger*. Its focus is on women and anger, but I recommend it to almost everyone. She covers many topics, among them boundaries, co-dependency, change and, of course, anger. In fact, she pretty much covers the waterfront. Thankfully, expressing emotions other than anger has become more socially acceptable for males. Unfortunately, women are often still seen differently than men when they express their anger.

We all come into this world equipped with Mother Theresa loving kindness, homicidal rage and every emotion in between. What we feel is never wrong or bad; it just *is*. When we look at behavior, the filter changes. When we say hurtful things we can never un-ring that bell. Therein lies the danger of speaking out of anger, yet being fallible human beings, each of us has had that experience. The expression "Sticks and stones can break our bones, but words can never harm us" is untrue. Words can do a lot of damage! To express our feelings in a way that makes them clear and understandable, we need to find tools to help our listeners hear our feelings without being blamed for them. If we call upon our feelings, our boundaries and our wise minds to determine our behavior, we are capable of finding ways of expression that are far more likely to foster a positive outcome than a negative one.

Of course anger is not the only challenging emotion we experience. According to Pia Mellody, Senior Clinical Advisor for The Meadows, the eight basic emotions are: anger, fear, pain, joy, passion, love, shame and guilt. Others (some of which are subsets of the above) include sadness, grief, envy, jealousy, greed, helplessness, loneliness, disgust, trust, anticipation, surprise and vulnerability. So often we're taught to 'stuff' our feelings, i.e. to not express them, or encouraged to believe we're wrong for feeling what we do. In Brene Brown's TED Talk, *Listening to Shame*, she talks about shame being linked to feelings about oneself. She states that "negative self-talk is born in shame," and indeed there is a strong connection between the two. She offers that guilt means 'I did something bad.' Shame, on the other hand, is equivalent to 'I *am* bad.' I agree with these definitions and believe that often people turn guilt into shame, i.e. 'I did something bad, and therefore I *am* bad.' Thankfully, our culture is now addressing feelings differently with young children as the primary target audience. It's fortunate that their parents also get to benefit from these important lessons.

When my children were growing up, there was a wonderful segment on Sesame Street called "Name that Feeling" in a game show format. I loved that, as it gave children an opportunity to learn about and 'name' feelings. The current children's programming is amazing, and it is another source of learning healthy ways of dealing with life, feelings and relationships. Both my granddaughter and I relished the movie *Inside Out*! 'Joy' was her favorite the day we went to the theatre to see the movie, and she dressed all in yellow and looked very much like the movie character—minus the blue hair! A few weeks after seeing the movie, 'Disgust' was her emotion of choice. Her ability and freedom to move from one preference and emotion to another with such ease is wonderful to see. We've come a long way.

A word of caution about numbing our feelings: if we numb the painful feelings, the good ones go right along with them. This strategy is often employed by people, and when this occurs, there is a flat quality to their lives. No highs or lows, but no feelings either. Generally they experience a sense of distress about this, but of course it's muted along with every other feeling. Numbing as a defense does not work well at all.

When we are young, we learn defense mechanisms to protect us from our difficult feelings, as well as from hurt inflicted by others. Most of these early defense mechanisms are by definition, primitive. The goal is that these will evolve into more sophisticated and healthier defenses as we grow up. The better our boundaries, the better able we are to take care of ourselves in many ways. Learning to soothe ourselves when we need soothing is very important for regulating our emotions. We will always have ourselves as a resource, and when we can provide what we need to ourselves we are not solely dependent upon others for comfort. This is a vital part of the individuation and independence process. Some of the more primitive defenses include denial, regression and acting out, to name a few. Some of the more evolved defenses include intellectualization, rationalization and repression, and believe it or not, humor!

Armed with understanding, our evolving defense system, emotional growth, and life experience, we also begin to evolve and to realize that we have choices, which may not have been apparent at earlier times—including undoing the messages we received about ourselves, when necessary. Not only can we re-write our script, we can throw the whole thing out and start over again with our own version! What a somewhat scary but incredibly empowering idea that is.

* * *

Breaking Free

Not Doing What You're Told

Fast forward to adulthood and to the messages we've held on to as fact from childhood without reconsideration: we now *believe* those negative messages. We hear them as our own inner voice and as truth. We weren't born with that truth. We developed it through the messages we received, whether or not we interpreted them correctly. Now it's time to look at what to do with all that 'stuff.' We'll begin by getting our feet wet at the shallow end of the pool. It won't take too long for the waters to deepen, however.

Some people are able to start breaking free at earlier ages. For many others, it doesn't occur until adulthood. When we really start to look at those negative messages we have the opportunity to begin the change process.

Choosing a path not considered to be popular brings me to a saying of which I'm very fond: 'Other people's opinions of me are none of my business.' Internalizing this is a difficult thing to achieve. We are highly influenced by others' opinions of us. Trusting that our own opinion is the one that counts the most is a process requiring time and effort. I don't believe we're ever totally immune from the opinions of others, especially those closest to us. Sometimes that's a good thing. We just might be missing something. For the most part, however, our own truth is the one that matters most.

Almost all of my clients have a really difficult time with the next premise, as did I, the first time I heard it. Here goes. If there are two people in the room and one of them *has* to get hurt, make sure it's not you! The exceptions for me are my kids. I see my granddaughter emerging as my third exception. They're the ones I'd take that bullet for. When it comes to potential harm, my instinct will always be to protect them at my expense. As for the rest: 'First, me.' This is an extension of the airplane and oxygen metaphor—taking care of oneself first. To soften it a bit, I'd like to add my belief that taking care of yourself truly takes care of more than just yourself. That's more often the truth than not.

In the late nineties I had the privilege of co-leading a women's therapy group with another female psychotherapist. The dynamic in this group was very interesting, as we had the luxury of being completely open about women, as well as our perceptions of men. During the course of this group our unanimous dislike for being seen as 'Sugar and spice and everything nice' arose as a topic. Years ago, this was an often repeated characterization describing what little girls are made of. The subject of being nice was one we questioned with great intensity. One of the group members brought in: "The Price of Nice" from *Creative Aggression* by Dr. George R. Bach and Dr. Herb Goldberg. I owe them a debt of gratitude for this brilliant exposé debunking the myth that being nice is a good thing. According to Bach and Goldberg, there is a price to pay for both the nice person and others involved with them. Being nice requires suppressing negative feelings and interferes with intimacy because it is not emotionally authentic. It is therefore impossible to trust the nice person, and relationships suffer as a result. In short, without intimacy, authenticity and trust, both the nice person and those he or she relates to lose.

In our group we determined that being nice was highly overrated. We were left with a puzzle to solve about what we *did* want to be, and we came to the conclusion that what we really wanted was to be *kind*. Understanding the difference between the two is very important. Some helpful tips are to be found in the wise words of a therapist friend of mine. If you have something difficult to say or for your listener to hear, ask yourself three questions: is it honest, is it kind, and is it necessary? When I heard this I immediately wondered for whom was it necessary, and my friend replied, "For either or both." At times being honest in this context can be extremely difficult, but in the end, it is most often the better choice.

If you don't say the truth that needs to be spoken, are you doing the other person a service or a disservice? For example, let's say you have a close friend or relative who treats you in manner you perceive as disrespectful. If you don't tell them, you'll likely wind up wanting to avoid them. You may not be the only one. Is it kind not to tell them? I don't believe so. I do believe it's difficult to say and difficult to hear. If you recall, one of the three questions was, "Is it necessary?" In this case, in my opinion, it is. Your goal is to say it in the easiest way for them to hear, which means without blame or judgment. Clearly, this wouldn't be considered 'nice,' although it would be kind. Of course, it's always a good idea to ask permission after telling someone you have something to share that might be difficult for you both, but which you, yourself would want to know. I refer to this concept as 'knocking before entering.' It's an important way of respecting someone's boundaries.

I'm also a fan of tooting your own horn. We are taught not to do this. It's kind of like 'selfish'—another thing we're not supposed to be or do. After a certain point in childhood it becomes unacceptable to many. While it might be okay for little Teddy, the kindergartener, to come home and proudly proclaim, "Look at the beautiful picture I made!" It doesn't take too long for Teddy to be told that "bragging is bad," so let others tell you those things about yourself. Socially, of course, we cannot go around proclaiming our greatness to all we see; however, there is a middle ground about which we are generally ignorant. I'm reminded of John, who started an Internet business on the side of his day job. He told practically no one about this venture, as it felt too self-serving to him. I asked him how he expected people to find out about his business. He realized and acknowledged that he was standing in his own way, and that he could make a different choice. This behavior frequently occurs.

And while we're on the subject of not doing what you're told, let's talk about having and using your voice, finding and claiming your inner truth, standing your full height, and self-esteem. Oh, and let's not forget owning your power! One word of caution I want to add to the subject of power is to say that once you claim it, it's important to use it both wisely and appropriately and to trust your gut to let you know if you're not.

The notion of having and using your voice seems like it would just come naturally. Unfortunately this is often not the case. People often fail to speak up for the sake of peace at any price, not wanting to be judged by others, fear of others' reactions and a multitude of other reasons—fear most often being a part of it. This can be seen across the board, although it may be especially reserved for relationships with those closest to us. When we don't have a voice, we have no power. It is essential to find and claim your voice in order to reclaim your power. We all deserve to be heard.

I find it both interesting and encouraging that many of these themes are being reflected in pop and other music. The voice of music is carrying those messages, and it is a potent and evocative voice. Music makes us feel.

Looking briefly at how greatly the musical message has changed over time, we have only to recall the hit from the Broadway musical Guys and Dolls, *Sit Down, You're Rockin' the Boat* with its literal admonition not to make waves, along with dire consequences should one do so. Things started to change, and making waves not only became acceptable, but desirable in one of the first songs to commemorate Women's Liberation, *I Am Woman*, written and performed by Helen Reddy and on her album *I Don't Know How to Love Him.* That same concept of roaring was woven into a more recent example by Katy Perry in her song entitled—you guessed it—*Roar.* Speaking up often requires courage, but it can certainly lead to being your own champion and rocking the boat when necessary. The experience of being heard is of utmost importance—not only for women, but for men, as well. It is not only important for adults, but equally so for children who often feel they do not have a voice or a choice. A roar is most definitely a loud proclamation of having a voice.

Yet another example is the popular song by Sarah Bareilles, *Brave.* Again, it takes courage to say the hard things, but so often, the results are better for both the person who says what they want and need to say and for the one who hears them.

And finally (for now), the words from the song, *Let it Go*, from the movie *Frozen* sung by Idina Menzel, has been a 'homework assignment' I ask my clients to listen to, for although the character is speaking to the specifics of the story, the message is much broader and an important one for us all. *Be yourself, don't hide your feelings and power, don't worry about what others will say, and don't be controlled by what scares you.*

Failure to speak up often breeds resentment. As difficult as feeling guilty is, it's easier to overcome than resentment, which tends to settle in and build over time. I've seen this phenomenon many times, so I believe if it's a choice between saying something about which you might feel guilty, or not saying something about which you might feel resentment, choose guilt. Once you've discovered that you have a voice and decide to use it, remember the three questions. (Is it honest, kind and necessary?)

Finding and claiming your inner truth is simply being in touch with your gut, your wisdom and your emotions. When these three are brought together, your truth is readily apparent. Most often, people ignore their gut and go straight to their brain or emotions. While I'm all for using your wise mind, as well as a strong supporter of emotional awareness, it is imperative to engage all three parts of yourself. Then it becomes incumbent upon us to speak from and act from the combination of these. I was intrigued to learn about the vagus nerve. This nerve corresponds with 'gut,' so it is a real physiological phenomenon. The vagus nerve conveys information directly to the brain, both from the abdomen and the heart. All three are in communication with each other at all times, regardless of what our brains may want us to believe. Only by using all three parts of ourselves can we maximize our ability to know ourselves and to act and react from a place of authenticity. That's pretty awesome!

Most of us have a 'go-to' place in times of stress or conflict. It's usually cognitive or emotional and sometimes power. If emotion is our go-to place, it takes real work to re-engage our brain along with the feelings. We often act and speak from an emotional place without a filter or consideration of how our words impact another. This is human; however, it seldom ends well. Just like I recommend bringing your adult back on board when one of your child parts is running the show, I also recommend re-engaging your brain when your emotions have taken over. Similarly, if you are all about what's in your head, it is extremely helpful to get in touch with what you are feeling. I often see people trying to communicate when one is operating from their emotions and the other from their cognition. Successful communication is usually impossible under those circumstances. They are literally speaking two different languages. Sometimes this is seen when one person is looking at the logic of the situation at the same time the other is all about the feelings being experienced. An example might be a father telling his daughter how he felt hurt that she didn't contact him on his birthday. She responds by saying that her phone died. In this instance, she is focused on logic as opposed to being able to hear and respond to her father's hurt.

Pay attention to your gut (or vagus nerve), stay with it for a while, notice what you are feeling, and then finally determine your thoughts. As you probably already know, this is not easy and takes a lot of practice, but the results are so much better. Another useful practice is to take at least several deep, slow breaths. When we are in a highly emotional state, it is common for people to hold their breath. Doing so prevents oxygen from entering the brain, which needs oxygenation in order to work properly! To use an expression I recently heard and like very much, "Stand still, don't hurry up."

Standing your full height is very closely related to self-esteem. It's holding onto yourself with the clear knowledge that you are entitled to be who you are, to not cower in fear or perpetually give in to what others want. This does not mean that you are so entitled that other people don't matter, rather it takes into account and makes certain that you are consistently and fairly represented. Or, as Kelly Clarkson suggests in the song *Catch My Breath*, we are our own arbiters of truth. She's obviously an advocate of breathing, as well! And even more radical are the lyrics by OneRepublic in *Counting Stars*, in which they refer to claiming one's authenticity despite social pressure to conform and in *Renegades* by X Ambassadors who speak of underdogs, outlaws, and yes, breaking the rules!

Many would call this rebellious, and I acknowledge there may be some of that; however, I don't think that's a bad thing. My suggestion is that if we buy into someone else's opinion of us, we must utilize 'auto correct' and remind ourselves that 'Other people's opinions of me are none of my business.'

Self-esteem is essential to our well-being. So often I hear people say about someone else that he or she has a big ego. I generally respond by saying, "No, in fact he or she probably has a small ego. People who feel good about themselves do not find it necessary to proclaim their value to the world, nor to do it at the expense of others. It is those people who need to find validation from others who engage in that practice." Now you might ask, how is that different from tooting your own horn? That's a very good question.

Acknowledging your abilities and accomplishments is very different from treating other people in a manner suggesting that your abilities and accomplishments are better than theirs. That's more like being a know-it-all, a trait no one finds attractive. So when people say someone has a big ego, they are not complimenting the person to whom they are referring. How does this differ from self-esteem? Vastly. When you esteem yourself, value who you are and have no doubt about your worth as a human being, it comes across to others in a very positive manner. Bragging is neither desirable nor necessary, but acknowledging yourself and your worth is both.

Fear and admonition (again from our childhood 'script') is what holds us back perhaps the most. People often fear that they will go to the opposite extreme if they let go of the extreme they're already at. For example, the perfectionist fears they'll stop caring about doing anything worthwhile, the pessimist fears they'll lose what they consider to be 'control' over not being surprised by negative events, which is only an illusion, after all, and the person who is always helping others fears they will help no one again. Might we swing like a pendulum at first when trying out new behaviors? Yes, it does happen on occasion. But guess what? We don't stay there long, as it is never a comfortable resting place.

Your mission is to find a sense of love and respect for yourself, and to be able to describe yourself in the same glowing terms you'd use for someone you love. I promise you will not 'get a big head,' become a braggart, be 'too big for your britches,' think you're better than everyone else, or become 'a legend in your own mind.' There is no negative price attached to loving oneself, only positive outcomes.

● ● ●

Self-Actualization

Abraham Maslow, an important leader in personality theories who helped develop humanistic psychology, is widely known as having defined the term 'self-actualization.' His development of this concept was influenced by German neurologist and psychiatrist, Kurt Goldstein who introduced it in 1939. Maslow stated that, "human motivation is based upon people seeking fulfillment and change through personal growth." Self-actualized people were those who were fulfilled and doing all they were capable of. "The growth of self-actualization refers to the need for personal growth and discovery present throughout a person's life." He contends that "a person is always 'becoming' and never remains static. In self-actualization, a person discovers an important meaning to their life."

One of the things I appreciate most about his theory is that he departed from the usual path of focusing on what goes wrong with people to focus on what goes right. He believed that "emotional peaks occur when experiencing the world totally for what it truly is which results in feelings of euphoria, joy and wonder. This is different for each person," as is the focus, i.e. being good at something in which we place value although it's not necessarily what someone else values.

Maslow delineated "behaviors leading to self-actualization, such as being fully absorbed in life with a child's wonder, listening to your inner voice and feelings, trying new pathways, being your authentic self, taking responsibility and being willing to work toward goals, and identifying your defenses" and finding the courage to let them go.

When people begin the change process and begin to let go not only of fear but of their more primitive defenses, I always urge caution to proceed at a comfortable pace, and to not throw away all defenses until they've got some healthier ones to replace the old ones. As with most things regarding change, this process does require courage.

In *The Right to be Human: A Biography of Abraham Maslow*, Edward Hoffman states: "It is important to note that self-actualization is a continual process of becoming rather than a perfect state one reaches of a 'happy ever after.'" Maslow said of his list that it's not necessary to display all the above characteristics. I subscribe to this definition of self-actualization and its importance. In conjunction with therapy, I believe that both are often ongoing processes, sometimes with breaks in between, as we encounter new periods of growth, as well as life's pitfalls and bumps. I so often repeat his words, "There are no perfect human beings," that I probably need to hang that quote on the wall of my office!

Another important book that sits in my waiting room is*: The Four Agreements: A Practical Guide to Personal Freedom* by Don Miguel Ruiz. The first and fourth Agreements are the most relevant to this section: Be Impeccable with Your Word and Always Do Your Best (with the understanding that your best will be different from time to time). Ruiz states that the first Agreement is the most important. The manner in which he focuses on each word of the Agreement edifies this concept, with a special emphasis on the power of 'word.' The second and third pertain to relationships more often than not, and they are: Don't Take Anything Personally and Don't Make Assumptions. Ruiz and I both agree that these four basic tenets are a guide to personal freedom and happiness.

● ● ●

I can think of no one better than Mark Twain to quote as I end this section:

"Life is short, Break the Rules.
Forgive quickly, Kiss SLOWLY.
Love truly. Laugh uncontrollably.
And never regret ANYTHING
That makes you smile."

Part Two

Then You

"Never allow someone to be your priority while allowing yourself to be their option."

—*Unknown*

Who's Next?

As we begin to look at 'You,' remember that it's extremely important that this addition doesn't displace or cause the 'Me' to disappear. Hold on to this concept of keeping the 'Me' intact as you go forward.

For most of us, the first 'you' is our mothers. Sometimes it's our fathers and sometimes a combination of both. This combination is more frequently found in the parenting of today; however, for simplicity's sake I will refer to mothers.

Mother's Day

The idea of putting Mother second doesn't have to enter an infant's mind—it is totally instinctual. When a baby is hungry, wet, and just generally wanting or needing something, there is no thought as to whether or not it might inconvenience someone to meet their needs. If that were the case, there would be no two a.m. feedings! Does that make the infant selfish? Well no, they are just doing what comes naturally.

If it is natural and instinctive for us to put our needs first, why must we consider that to be a bad thing as we get older? This occurs during the 'civilizing' process all children must undergo. Watching toddlers on the playground is an interesting example of the at times generosity and oftentimes ruthlessness with which children pursue their goals. If you are in the swing I want to be in, I might just stand in your way until you get off it. If I am bigger than you and you want to climb the ladder for the slide, I'm very likely to push you aside, climb first and say, "You can follow me."

Although we might chastise our children when they behave in this way, it is generally with an understanding that this is where they are. In other words, most parents will not judge their children. They might suggest different behavior, but hopefully not with censure.

This begins to change as toddlers grow older—once again, that 'civilizing' process. When it occurs, parents recognize the necessity for teaching their children that being completely egocentric is not socially acceptable or good for them. This is where the practice of mindlessly looking out only for oneself begins to change and becomes reshaped. Clearly, some of this is necessary to lay the groundwork for being able to see beyond one's own needs and wants and learn to consider the other person. It speaks to the concept of being 'centered in self' while introducing the need for awareness of the 'other.' This delicate balance often veers off beyond the idea of self-care into the benefits of other-care, usually reinforced by praise, lack of negative feedback and overall positive reinforcement from the 'other.' Here begins our first glimpse into substituting 'First Me' with 'First You.' To the extent this becomes reinforced, the child may begin to lose sight of the awareness of self and learn to instead focus on other.

The ideal is a balance between loving oneself and being increasingly able to prioritize one's needs and wants without throwing out concern for the other. It is still 'First Me.' If children receive negative input about self-love and self-care, they begin to internalize this input from others and experience it as 'truth' about themselves. This is where negative self-talk is born.

Unfortunately, there are many instances in which this process becomes reversed by the parent, who sends a message indirectly telling the child that the parent's need comes first. Given the importance and power Mother possesses, this reversal is all but impossible for the child to resist.

Jenny's parents are divorced, and her mother has not remarried. Mom doesn't date and has no male relationship in her life. She also has no close friends nor confidantes, so she turns to Jenny to get most of her needs met. This dynamic existed early in Jenny's life with her mom, so as Jenny grows older, it represents an increased level of an old dance. Jenny feels extremely burdened by her mother's needs. She cannot refuse to meet them because to do so would cause her to feel guilty that she was abandoning her mother. She is also not confident that her mother can take care of herself without Jenny's involvement. Jenny is emotionally enslaved, and 'Then You' cannot apply until Jenny is able to emotionally separate from her mom and learn to take care of herself instead of her mother, whatever the consequences for both.

It's important to understand that before we can be emotionally separate, we must first be connected. Connection is a vital part of what people need and seek. It's inherent in all of us. Obviously, connection is a very positive thing. We first experience it physically in the womb. We next experience it with our primary caregivers. The need for autonomy does not begin to solidify until we are able to distinguish and assert our own needs and wants within that connected relationship. Then, in conjunction with our need for separateness, we retain the need for connectivity. Once again, the balance between the two must exist and remain somewhat fluid. In a sense, we are in part returning to our original alliance with self. When I speak of individuation and separation, I want to be clear that the goal is to foster our own identity without precluding the essential sense of being connected. With whom we are connected and when is a part of this process. To the extent that we have the ability to determine that for ourselves, we will benefit from both the connection and the separation.

Sometimes our parents do not let us go. In those instances, it is very difficult for the child (be they adult or younger) to be the one to make that separation happen; however, it is essential that we do so. If we fail to separate from our families of origin to become our own individual selves, we can never be fully functional or happy. It also interferes with our ability to properly attach and be loyal to the families that we create as adults.

One of the most frequent topics of conflict for couples occurs when one or both partners feel that their significant other's family comes before them. It is essential in a healthy relationship that one's partner holds a top priority, second only to ourselves. When our family of origin interferes with this paradigm, there will be trouble. Many people do not separate emotionally from their family of origin until they are in their thirties or older. Some are able to do it earlier, and some are even able to do it in a healthy way. This process is facilitated when parents encourage their adult children to have their own lives and to not make their parents their priority. My favorite expression for describing how we relate to our families of origin without becoming enmeshed is to suggest that my clients visit with their family sitting on the bank, instead of getting into the quicksand along with them. This is most often necessary when their family of origin is dysfunctional to a destructive point.

The chorus from Cross Canadian Ragweed's *17*, about how we become a younger version of ourselves when we go back home, pretty much hits the nail on the head. It seems very natural when we are with our families to fall back into our roles in the family. We start to see ourselves the way our family saw us and perhaps continues to see us. Introducing change into that environment is generally incumbent upon the person who wants the emotional separation to occur. When I speak of separation, I'm not suggesting cutting off relationships or not continuing to grow relationships, rather establishing adult to adult relationships with our families, especially our parents and siblings. An illustration of how some adult 'children' use therapy to help enable this process is Brenda, who brought her parents to therapy to talk about their relationships. Neither parent had been in therapy on their own. They weren't aware of Brenda's struggle to retain a relationship with them, while creating separation from them and the dysfunction in their family. Mom cried, and Dad got angry, which was exactly what Brenda had both predicted and feared. I told them that I've noticed that we parents tend to credit our children with all that goes well for them, and blame ourselves when it doesn't. That irony (and truth) is seldom lost on parents. As the session progressed, Mom and Dad were finally able to 'hear' their adult daughter telling them how important they were to her. They also heard how important it was to her for them to support her independence from them, without anyone feeling blamed or unloved. As is usually the case, this occurred after Brenda had dealt with her own issues around emotional separation from her parents. She was prepared for the possible negative fallout and able to deal with it while remaining in her 'adult self.' All walked out of my office gratified by how the meeting had gone.

There is an inevitable protectiveness we all feel toward our parents, no matter how they treated us. As I discussed earlier, the abused child will almost always want to return to the abusive parent if given a choice. This bond goes so deep, it is my belief that it can never be severed. "Step on a crack and break your mother's back" is a saying with which almost everyone is familiar. How many of us spent a lot of time in our childhoods avoiding cracks at all costs? This behavior, although not literally, most often continues into adulthood. We may lash out at our parents, but it costs us dearly. We feel extreme guilt and believe we've damaged or betrayed our parents in irreparable ways—particularly with our mothers. I often refer to mothers as unrelenting steam rollers until we turn around and suggest they stop rolling, at which point they suddenly dissolve into fragile flowers whom we have wounded beyond measure. Clearly, this is a terrible bind in which to find oneself, yet it is a common occurrence.

Considering all these factors makes it easier to see the challenge of emotionally separating from one's parents and family of origin. I can't emphasize enough how essential it is that this take place. The best way to be close with another person is to be separate from them. This may sound like a contradiction, however it is not. You can't be close if you are part of the same whole, e. g. "I feel really, really close to my arm." Despite the absurdity inherent in that statement, the premise is sound. When I speak of separation, I am, at the same time, speaking of developing a close, loving and caring relationship. Sometimes this is not possible, depending upon our parent's ability and willingness to engage in such a relationship with us. In such a situation, we can only do the best we can.

If we change our 'dance,' the other person in relationship with us can no longer continue the old dance. Bill's mother, also without emotional resources and people in her life, wants to talk to him about her life, her sorrows, her woes, etc. As she ages, the frequency and repetition of her litany increases, and his frustration only grows stronger. His sister has distanced herself from their mother for this reason. The more Bill's sister moved out of the picture, the more he felt responsible for his mother and her happiness. Over time, Bill came to the realization that he was entitled to set limits with his mother and to only listen to the extent that it was not stressful for him to do so. He finally recognized and respected *his own* boundaries. This promoted his willingness to interact with her, as he knew he could stop when he needed to take care of himself without feeling guilty. To again utilize the dance metaphor, Bill and his mom were doing a waltz. When he stopped waltzing and began to cha-cha, she could no longer waltz *with him.* If she wanted to continue to relate to him, she'd have to dance the cha-cha. Bill's mother had no wish to lose their relationship, so she adapted as best she could. I would refer to Bill as a 'change agent' for his family. Very often the adult 'child' introduces behaviors and ideas to their family, which effectively change the family dynamic. If they are growing, these changes are for the better! In time, perhaps his sister will see the changes and re-enter their mother's life. If that happens, not only will she and her mother benefit, but so will Bill. The responsibility might become something he can share with her. This applies in any relationship when what we are doing or participating in is not serving our own best interests. Remember 'First Me!'

The Other 'Kids'

After our parents, the 'you' will take many forms. 'You' might be a sibling, a friend, a relative, or a boyfriend/girlfriend, etc. Many children grow up taking care of siblings. This behavior can extend well into adulthood and is inevitably accompanied by resentment and guilt. That doesn't mean we don't love our sibling; however, taking care of them is a burden. Once we learn in our families of origin to take care of the other before ourselves, we are more likely to continue this behavior in all of our relationships. 'First Me' gets lost in the shuffle. So many times I've heard people who were the oldest child express a sense of frustration and resentment about having had to include their younger siblings in activities, take care of their younger siblings while parents were away and fulfill more of a parental than sibling role—not to mention possibly feeling displaced and definitely having to share parental attention. This is usually accompanied by guilt, as well, since most people love their siblings. Sometimes roles are not dependent upon birth order. Circumstances may turn a younger child into the caregiver of an older sibling. At its extreme, it is not a healthy situation. It constitutes enabling, allowing the dependent sibling to grow up without the need to become independent and self-sufficient, and perhaps, without the confidence in their ability to do so. This is not beneficial for any adult who is capable of taking care of themselves. In the song, *Save Yourself*, Suzy Bogguss put it well when she referenced not being willing to drown while trying to rescue someone she cared about. The risk is always there, and it's important to keep in mind. That's why lifeguards swim sidestroke in the water, so they can keep both the person they're saving and themselves alive. Since most of us aren't lifeguards, it's not our job. Unless it fits our job description (e.g. nurse, doctor), we are not qualified to be saving someone else—let alone at our expense!

Thinking back to my own adolescence, I recall my best friend in junior high, Martha. We were very close, and we liked it that way! I remember one day when we deliberately wore identical outfits to school and were called into the gym teacher's office. She told us that dressing alike wasn't okay because we were each individuals, and by dressing the same we negated that. We just thought she was mean and spoiling our fun. Now I look back and wish I'd had the ability at thirteen to understand how important her message really was. As a therapist, I understand all too well that we can't hear what someone is saying until we are ready and able to do so.

Speaking of adolescence, never is there a time more fraught—both for adolescents and their parents! Life begins to radically change along with the adolescent brain, according to recent research. What we've attributed to hormones in the past is no longer seen as the explanation. A much heralded book and New York Times Bestseller *Brainstorm: The Power and Purpose of the Teenage Brain* by Daniel J. Siegel, M.D. explains this phenomenon and is written for both adolescents and parents alike, in a respectful manner that doesn't vilify adolescents in the way they are often portrayed. Beginning with these changes, the lines between 'First Me' and 'Then You' are often blurred, especially in relation to peers. For adolescents, moods tend to be mercurial at times, and their lives often don't feel in their control. Couple that with the sense of omnipotence (e.g. death will never happen to me) that is part of the stage, and it can be a regular roller coaster ride. Siegel refers to interdependence—a healthy model of both independence and dependence. It is often present in an adolescent's peer group and is a great precursor for a healthy loving partner relationship in adulthood, in which interdependence is such a key element. Adolescents are no longer 'children,' but still not adults, a conundrum for them, as well as the others in their lives.

Peer pressure is a frequently used term, especially among parents. Most children and adolescents are desirous of being just like (or better than) their peers, and never standing out as different unless it is in a positive light. They work hard to fit in, so, like Martha and me, they sometimes think obliterating their individuality is a good thing. Being 'cool' is a concept that seemingly never dies. *Cool Kids* by Echosmith is a recent example of this desire. Young people want to fit in, belong, and be popular without a care. Yet even 'the cool kids' are just as beset by their own insecurities, worries and fears as those who don't see themselves as 'cool.' Inside every adult lives that younger version of ourselves, and I doubt there is one among us, having been cool or not, who would disagree that it was a challenging time.

Once we pass beyond adolescence (yes, believe it or not, after twenty-four) and become young adults, it doesn't necessarily follow that we can keep our boundaries clear and move between 'first me' and 'then you' with ease. Old patterns persist. Our relationships with our families still carry a great deal of weight. Any relationships we form are still drawn from limited life experiences, simply because we haven't been around long enough to have had many of them or the opportunity to acquire the knowledge which goes along with them. As annoying a comment as it is, I *do* believe that mistakes are learning opportunities. That doesn't mean we like making them or enjoy the fallout from mistakes; it's just what makes us human, fallible and still capable of learning.

When Sharon was in her thirties, she despaired of ever being shed of the responsibility for her younger brother, whose life was largely comprised of drug addiction and subsequent legal ramifications. She loved her brother. But she worried about him and the burden he would become for her parents were she to step out of the role of caregiver. Through our sessions and the support of others in her life, Sharon gradually came to the realization that she was actually doing no one a service. She began to withdraw from the role of caregiver. Her parents agreed not take her place with their son. By doing so, all sent a message to him that although they loved him, his family was no longer willing to be responsible for him or continue to enable him. It took some time, but eventually her brother stepped up to the plate, got clean, found a job and got married. He began to live a productive life in which he took responsibility for himself. This process gave him the opportunity to gain a tremendous amount of confidence and self-esteem. As it turned out, Sharon's withdrawal from the role of caretaker was a gift she gave to herself and to her family. And no, it doesn't always have a happy ending. It does, however, maximize the possibilities for one.

Often quoted from Leviticus 19:18 is: "Love thy neighbor as thyself." I think there is an inherent assumption that we will love ourselves, while suggesting that we treat others with the same kindness and consideration we give to ourselves. I believe many people try to live up to the first part of this mandate. The part they so often miss, however, is 'thyself.' I wonder what would've happened if the quote had been "Love thyself, then love your neighbor in the same way." Would we have thought that it was our first job to love ourselves and our second job to love our neighbor? How might our lives be different? How might the world be different? Are 'selfies' an attempt to insert ourselves into our own lives and into that 'first' place? And would we need them if we were already there?

Madeline and Amy were best friends all the way through school. When I met Madeline, she was in a long-term unhappy, romantic relationship she couldn't seem to exit. She began to talk about her relationship with Amy, and the many similarities she was beginning to see in her current relationship with Tom. Although Madeline was independent in many ways, she chose to be in relationships with people who treated her as 'less than' themselves. She tolerated this treatment for the most part. She couldn't make sense of why she would be drawn to people who didn't appear to respect her. Upon looking at her childhood, the origin of this dynamic became clear, since this was how her father treated her. Because she had tried hard and long to win his respect and never succeeded, she had transferred this dynamic into her significant relationships with others. I offered Madeline a simple but invaluable truth: "We teach people how to treat us." When we tolerate ill treatment, disrespect, abuse, etc., we are in effect saying, "It's okay for you to treat me badly. I will accept it." This message is so often sent, that it speaks volumes in offering an explanation as to why people endure what to the outsider looks unendurable. When our boundaries are so permeable, there are no limits to what we might put up with. This idea of teaching other people how to treat us is one I fully embrace.

In order to change this, it's first important to recognize, as Madeline did, that when our gut is protesting about the treatment we're receiving, we would benefit from paying attention. Once attended to, we have the opportunity to decide we deserve something better by taking a long, hard look at ourselves. We might first wonder why we would tolerate disrespect, and then come to the likely conclusion that it's either an old habit or that we don't sufficiently esteem ourselves. In this instance, it's likely that the first led to the second and they go hand in hand. An important step toward gaining greater self-esteem is to recognize its lack. Then there is an opportunity for change. Affirmations, peer support and therapy are some tools which can help establish a healthy sense of worth. Once self-esteem increases, tolerance for ill treatment decreases, and we begin to teach others that they must treat us with the respect we now know we deserve.

As people become aware of what they're teaching people about how to treat them, they will be much more likely to fulfill the entire mandate to "Love thy neighbor *as thyself*."

Adolescent and Adult Significant Others

Let's move to relationships with significant others in adolescence and adulthood. If we think of these relationships as partnerships, it creates a space and an attitude for seeing three separate entities: me, you and us. Relationships don't work well when the individual becomes obliterated by the 'us.' Nor do they work well when we are each so separate and self-involved that there is no 'us.' The healthiest relationships are comprised of both. This lack of two separate individuals can manifest in a variety of ways. Very often people feel responsible for their partner. They take this job very seriously. They put their efforts into making their partner happy and making their partner's life better. Regrettably, they are doomed to fail because we cannot do this for someone else. We cannot take care of them, although we can care about them. We can't *make* them happy. I want to point out the very important difference between the concepts of being responsible and being responsive. When we are not attempting to be responsible for someone else, we are far better equipped to be responsive to them and to their needs and wants. This goal *is* attainable, and that's a good partial definition of interdependence. We can also care for them, but not attempt to *take care of* them, which allows for greater mutual independence, another essential ingredient for interdependence.

Susan Forward wrote about the "blinding FOG—fear, obligation, and guilt—that characterizes most 'toxic tie' relationships." These are unhappy and unhealthy feelings, primarily intended to avoid loss of the other at great expense. Another thing we cannot give to someone else is the belief that they are lovable. We may try, hoping if we love them enough they will finally believe it. Conversely, if we do not believe that we are lovable, it's inconceivable for us to truly believe that we are loved. It all begins with loving ourselves or, as

I've heard it put, "falling in love with myself." Only then can we know and believe we are worthy of the love of others.

Feeling unlovable may lead us to fears of abandonment by those we need. This may lead to desperation, as well as a seemingly compelling reason for giving away our power. Feeling responsible for someone else's feelings often accompanies this dynamic. If we can just be good enough, then perhaps they will love us and never leave. This idea of abandonment, according to author John Lee in *Growing Yourself Back Up*, is a regression. He states that children feel and can actually be abandoned, however adults are just 'left' and always have options. This is an important distinction.

When I speak of partnership in this context, I am referring to a loving partnership, not a business proposition. Wanting to help someone is well-intentioned and comes from a place of caring and goodwill in romantic partnerships, as well as other relationships. There is certainly no fault in this. Trouble often arises, however, when wanting to help becomes trying to fix. Stereotypically, wanting to fix someone else's problems is attributed to males, but women can certainly be included in this category. The difficulty arises because most of us, if we are healthy and independent, do not want someone else to fix our problems. We want to solve our own problems. This increases our confidence, self-esteem and 'self-actualization.' We may or may not welcome suggestions, input, support, understanding and empathy. None of those are fixes, but they can often be helpful to us. I give you the quintessential rejoinder of every two year old: "Me do it!" As we grow, we become less intractable, but it's still in there somewhere.

Now that we've looked at *who* we relate to, it's of vital importance to understand *how* we relate in the most constructive manner possible. This is the area where things are most likely to go awry unless we understand what's involved and how to deal with those complexities.

● ● ●

Boundaries

Essential to the concept of relating constructively are boundaries. They are necessary in all relationships. For our purposes I will use the following definition of boundaries: unofficial rules about what should not be done; limits that define acceptable behavior.

Most of us are aware that we have boundaries, some more conscious than others. Some examples of healthy boundaries include the following: being true to your own values and personhood, knowing yourself well enough to define, trust and hold on to your own truth, trusting others appropriately, saying no to anything unacceptable to you, clearly communicating your wants and needs, respecting other people's boundaries, taking responsibility for your own thoughts, feelings and actions, moving step-by-step rather than headlong into intimacy with another, and most importantly, treating yourself with love and respect.

Of the many books that have been written on this subject, I especially like the book, *Boundaries: Where You End and I Begin— How to Recognize and Set Healthy Boundaries* by Anne Katherine. One of my favorite parts of this book is the author's comparison between the boundaries of dogs and cats. She describes how when she comes home from work her dog rushes to her side and remains there. On the other hand, her cat might open one eye, see that she's home and then close it again. Like cats and dogs, different cultures have different physical boundaries. People often notice when they are speaking with someone from a different country or a different culture, that the person may stand closer to them than they are comfortable with or further away than they are accustomed to. Not all people nor all cultures share the same physical boundaries.

When it comes to relationships, however, the recognition of others' and our own unhealthy boundaries is very important. Remaining conscious of our healthy boundaries is important as well.

It's so important to maintain and respect one's own boundaries, while respecting those of others. Inherent in this concept is the protection of one's boundaries, while simultaneously extending the same concern for protection to someone else. Although this may sound like stating the obvious, all too often people lose sight of this essential concept. There is a reason that, 'You wouldn't say that to a stranger,' and 'You always hurt the one you love' have become song lyrics, as well as clichés. We often treat those closest to us with the least respect and without recognizing that we are violating their boundaries. Unfortunately, this is most often true in relationships with significant others and with our children and parents. Clearly, this can do a great deal of damage.

As we look at how we relate to others, we must first be certain that we have our boundaries firmly in place so that we interact from a position of safety for ourselves and others.

● ● ●

How We Relate To Others

Those Messy Emotions

What constitutes a healthy relationship with the people in our lives? We've looked at some ideas of how to define and go about that. Our culture, however, supports the notion that being a good family member, friend, partner, etc. means putting someone else's needs before our own, avoiding conflict, being faithful, being loyal and being respectful. I have no argument with the last three. About the first two, I have to disagree. Despite the fact that many believe differently, I must keep stating it repeatedly. In heterosexual romantic partnerships, there are women who become spokespeople for the concept of the man wearing the pants and the woman being in a follower role. I'm not sure too many men dare to espouse this concept currently, but it was certainly pervasive in the past. The implicit and sometimes explicit message here is for her to put his needs before hers. I must respectfully and strongly disagree. That said, each person and couple must determine the path that works best for them. In my paradigm, not only do I think the above disempowers women, I also think it burdens men. For me, this is not a gender-based concept either. Although male dominance has been the historical norm, there are couples in which the woman is the dominant party, and the man is the disempowered one. In same gender couples, either role may be taken on. Not all would agree with the idea of disempowerment either. If this works for the couple and both are satisfied, so be it. It's just not my model.

I've seen many women in my considerable years of practice who have 'lost themselves' or become 'de-selfed,' as Harriet Lerner so aptly terms it, in the process of putting their spouses in the driver's seat and literally taking a back seat—not even shotgun! Victoria tried to be the model (in her eyes) submissive wife and wound up in my office feeling so devoid of a self and so resentful of her husband, she couldn't figure out where to go from there. Over time, she was able to understand how much a loss of herself she'd experienced and to talk with her husband about it. Imagine her surprise when he eagerly accepted not only her message, but the opportunity to have a partner to share the burden! From there, it wasn't difficult for them to establish a new 'order' in which he didn't have all the responsibility, and she had an equal voice in determining what went on with herself, with them as a couple and with their family.

No relationship exists without its share of difficult and not-so-positive feelings. Those are the ones that can get us tangled up and into trouble. They include: anger, fear, shame, guilt, vulnerability, pain, grief, sadness, envy and jealousy. These get played out in many different ways by people.

For many, anger is the most difficult. Couples often refer to having conflict as arguing, fighting (most commonly), having a temper, being mean, yelling, being abusive, etc. None of these sounds like fun. Nor do they sound like methods for resolving conflict. In fact, most, if not all, are more likely to perpetuate and accelerate the level of conflict.

Most of us never learn how to resolve conflict. We are hardly ever taught how to express anger appropriately, and in fact, are most often taught not to express anger at all. Once again, I reiterate that the three hardest things we have to do in life we are not taught to do: take loving care of ourselves, have healthy relationships and parent children. I can't recall how many times I've heard someone describe themselves as being yelled at by their partner and had their partner deny the accusation while both were sitting in the room with me. What I frequently observe is that the person is not yelling, they just sound angry. Sounding angry is equated with yelling, being mean and being abusive on many occasions. It stands to reason that sounding angry is inevitable if one is angry. I also believe that hearing someone's anger can be frightening, upsetting and hurtful. This is because we equate anger with bad intentions and lack of love—even with hatred, at times. This equation is false. Sometimes people have bad intentions and sometimes people lack love. However, these are not synonymous with anger. This is such an important concept to learn and, once learned, can lead to very different and much more effective communication.

Many people cannot say they are angry—to do so might cause them to see themselves as 'the bad guy' or possibly culminate in the loss of a relationship. They can say they are irritated, annoyed, frustrated, etc., but the 'A' word seems forbidden. All these feelings exist on a continuum, mild irritation or annoyance being at one end and rage at the other. Whatever we call it, it bears a striking resemblance to anger, and since feelings are judgment proof, it's really okay to own one's anger. Anger can also serve as a great cover for vulnerability. Showing vulnerability is almost always scary. For those who can own their anger, it's much 'safer' to launch an 'attack' than it is to expose their vulnerabilities. This is both understandable and sad. It interferes with the recipient's ability to hear what's really going on with them, which often stems from pain. We react very differently to someone's pain than we do to their anger. To make things even more difficult, vulnerability is often equated with weakness. They are not the same thing, despite the fact that many hold to that belief. In her TED Talk, *The Power of Vulnerability*, Brene Brown says vulnerability is a measure of courage, and I concur. Our vulnerability reveals our authentic self. The risk is that the other won't accept us for who we are or will judge us and find us unacceptable and unlovable. Nevertheless, finding the courage to reveal this is necessary for a real connection between two real people, and if someone can love us even with our flaws exposed, it's incredibly affirming and a great way to get past our shame. If we never test that, we must keep at least part of who we really are hidden, and that limits both us and our relationship. *Locked Away* by R. City with Adam Levine is a touching song which basically asks this very question: would the love still be there if the flaws and vulnerability were shown?

If I stub my toe and it hurts, I'm likely to utter an expletive in a very angry tone of voice. I'm angry that I hurt myself, and I'm angry that I'm hurting. I'm not necessarily angry at anyone, unless they deliberately caused the toe to be stubbed, although I might get angry if someone accidentally stepped on my toe, and I might even direct my anger toward them, despite the fact it was an accident.

Anger is an emotion and therefore, by definition, irrational. We can get angry when something is not someone else's fault. Hopefully, once I come to my senses and my toe stops hurting so badly, I will apologize for directing my anger inappropriately toward the person who accidentally stepped on it. But, I'm entitled to not be happy that my toe still hurts. I often use this example to validate feelings that occur when we are hurt by someone who did not intend to hurt us. They probably feel bad that we are hurt by what they did. Most of the time people tell me that they are not entitled to their feelings if the other person is blameless. I submit that we are *always* entitled to our feelings. Our feelings belong to us, and again, they are judgment proof. There is, however, an important distinction to make when it comes to communicating feelings. No one else can 'make' us feel anything. Period. When someone says "that makes me feel…" 'that' is a euphemism for 'you.' They are not only failing to take responsibility for their own feelings, but are also placing blame on the other person, even if unintentionally. Our emotional response may be in keeping with the situation, but it is always our own. Since most of us are accustomed to this phrasing, I suggest becoming aware and working to change what we say and how we say it. We own our feelings; they belong to us.

Let's tackle what I think is the most painful feeling—shame. I describe shame as an annihilating feeling—the one that makes us want to disappear from sight. All of us have experienced it, and it's never a place we want to go to again. In her vulnerability TED Talk, Brown makes it clear that hiding the things we feel shame about makes the shame intensify. Carl Jung referred to shame as a 'soul eating emotion.' I think that does a potent job of explaining its power to harm us. My metaphor for this is that if you've got something hidden under a rock, when you move the rock and expose it to sunlight, it loses its power. Shame and secrecy often go together, but when we can share the secret and still be accepted by the listener, it lessens or eliminates the shame. One of the things I frequently tell my clients about therapy is that it offers people an opportunity to show someone who they really are and discover that the 'someone' does not run away shrieking in horror. In other words, the person is accepted for whom they are and continued to be valued. For many, therapy is the first place people can feel safe enough to try this out. Some never do, which is unfortunate both in terms of what they fail to gain and the pain they feel by continuing to hold onto the shame and secrecy. Many who do take the risk are able to expand this to other relationships. The therapeutic relationship is a microcosm of other relationships—a safe place to practice doing the hard stuff. Shame is the biggest risk we face when exposing our vulnerability. In order to get there, we have to manage another difficult emotion—fear.

Fear can be both a help and a hindrance. Fear protects us from real danger, and in that way its absence can harm us. One of the clearest examples of this is seen often in adult survivors of childhood sexual abuse. Because the boundaries were so violated in childhood, the adult antennae are often unable to pick up danger signs. So, it increases the risk to the person, and often leads to subsequent experiences of violation and assault. A number of years ago I was working in an office complex that shared a parking lot with a retail store. The store closed and a bar opened in that space, which significantly changed the perception of safety in the parking lot.

The people who were invested in the offices brought a lawsuit to evict the tenants in the bar, claiming it was detrimental to their business. I was subpoenaed to testify by their attorneys to confirm that I was concerned for both my clients and myself when in the parking lot at night. I told the attorney representing the bar that because I worked with many women who were adult survivors of sexual abuse, both my clients and I were distinctly uncomfortable. For a long time, I've been aware of the legal mandate to lawyers: never ask a question to which you don't know the answer. The attorney asked me if it wasn't true that abuse survivors would be quicker to experience danger when it didn't really exist. My answer was, "No, the opposite is true. They are less likely to sense danger and therefore more vulnerable to being victimized." The case was won, and I'm guessing that lawyer learned a couple of valuable lessons in the process. Fear can be a good thing, which protects us.

The hindrance side of fear not only feels uncomfortable, but can be limiting. It causes emotional and physical distress. We may avoid things that might be good for us to confront (e.g. vulnerability), and it can get in the way of optimal functioning. Phobias are often problematic for people, especially when the source is something frequently encountered. Phobias like arachnophobia (fear of spiders) don't occur every day, but might cause someone to avoid an activity in which a spider might be present. On the other hand, agoraphobia, (an excessive fear of being in crowds, public places or open areas) can be so extreme that the person cannot even leave their home. Thus, such an individual would be limited in their ability to lead a healthy life and develop healthy relationships. Oftentimes phobias are 'a place to hide' for a multitude of anxieties. It's as if those anxieties coalesce and attach to one specific fear. The good news is that phobias can be treated and resolved in many instances.

A very common 'cousin' to fear is anxiety. If people are having attacks over it, we can readily see what an intense and debilitating feeling it can be. Anxiety and depression are the two most often given reasons why people seek therapy for themselves. Significant levels of anxiety can severely limit a person's ability to function altogether. A lower level of anxiety causes distress, although quite often people are not aware of what the underlying feeling is, and frequently 'self-medicate' with alcohol, other substances, food, sex, exercise, etc. Although those tactics may reduce the anxiety, they do not address the causation. That's where therapy and self-exploration become invaluable tools to discover the cause.

Depression itself is not a feeling, but a state of mind and being. Depression is defined as a condition of general emotional dejection and withdrawal; sadness greater and more prolonged than that warranted by any objective reason. It's a combination of many feelings such as sadness, hopelessness and helplessness, and is often accompanied by anxiety. In fact, those two things (depression and anxiety) are often opposite sides of the same coin.

Grief is easily mistaken for depression, and the two may go hand in hand. Sometimes they defy separation. It's important to know that if we are grieving or depressed, we may suffer similar pain. Making the distinction becomes less important than working through the grief to then determine if the depression is resolved as well. Being sad doesn't necessarily constitute depression, even though when we are depressed, we are sad. Emotional pain can be comprised of any of the feelings mentioned before. It isn't unusual for our unconscious mind to 'speak up' by manifesting pain in our bodies. For example, Jennifer is prone to breaking bones, especially her ankles and toes. Knowing Jennifer, I believe it is her body's way of saying, "I just can't stand this!" Or, we might consider Todd's ongoing neck problems in light of the fact that he feels he carries the weight of the world on his shoulders (his words).

Despite the fact that envy and jealousy are used interchangeably, the difference between the two is important to understand. The word most commonly used for both is 'jealous.' Even the Bible says that envy (referred to as coveting in the Ten Commandments) is a bad thing, so it's not surprising that people are so reluctant to use the word. I believe we have shame about envy, in part because we are violating a Biblical tenet. Therefore, we remove it from our vocabulary. Even different dictionaries vary on the proper definition of jealousy. I found one in a British dictionary which nailed it: suspicious or fearful of being displaced by a rival. Some examples of jealousy include sibling rivalry—fear that the sibling is more loved by parents, and fear that a loved one will care more for another person. Jealousy boils down to fear of loss of love and importance. So if lexicographers have a problem with the definition, no wonder the rest of us do!

The dictionary defines envy as a feeling of discontent or *covetousness* with regard to another's advantages, success, possessions, etc. Some examples of envy are: a friend who inherits a fortune; a person whom we deem better looking or a better parent, athlete, etc. Similar to jealousy, this represents a feeling of loss. However it also constitutes more specific points of focus and is less about love than of things or attributes. Yes, it is 'coveting.' Is there anyone who is immune from this emotion? Highly doubtful. It's back to the fact that we are all human beings capable of all feelings that are—you guessed it—judgment-proof.

Interestingly, the dictionary also classifies jealousy and envy as synonyms; however, I believe there are some clear distinctions, as stated previously. Whatever we call it, it doesn't feel good. Perhaps it's helpful to think of envy as something we can do, whereas jealousy is something we have. For example, "I envy you for having such a great wife" as opposed to, "I'm jealous of my wife's interest in another man." Other not-so-good feelings include helplessness, vulnerability, hopelessness, etc. I believe that, as with many things in life, we have to 'take the bitter with the sweet.' If it was possible for us to only feel the 'good' feelings, it would likely limit our growth. Before deciding to try to eradicate the 'not-so-good' ones (an impossible task), do keep that in mind, as well as remembering that if we numb the 'bad' feelings, the 'good' go right along with them.

Let's take a look at some feelings which are positive. Appreciation is a wonderful thing to experience. I recently heard someone say that instead of complaining about traffic, it would be great if we could tell ourselves how lucky we are to live someplace that so many people want to live in, so therefore the traffic. It's a unique idea, yet I think it's quite a stretch for most.

Similar to appreciation is gratitude. I remember reading a poster in a doctor's office many years ago, written by a woman in her eighties, "Every day when I get up I have the option to feel bad about the parts of my body which don't work as well as they used to, or to be grateful for the ones that still do." I love that one—and it definitely speaks to gratitude!

Feelings such as joy, passion and love, as good as those sound, would not seem to be a source of difficulty; however, some people are uncomfortable with those feelings. Often, this occurs because they don't feel deserving of them or because they've numbed all their negative/difficult feelings, and as stated, when that happens, the good are also numb. A common example of discomfort with something positive is when people are unable to accept a compliment. So many of us find it difficult to just say, "Thank you," instead of qualifying why we don't think we're entitled to the compliment or dismissing it in some other fashion. "Your hair looks great!" is responded to with, "No, I really need to wash it." We don't intend to be dismissive of what the other said. Most of us are so accustomed to this type of response that we don't take it personally. However, it really *is* dismissive. How wonderful if we could recognize our response as discrediting what the other person said and refrain from doing so. Instead, we focus on our discomfort with receiving the 'good news.' This realization might provide a pathway to looking at why we can't just accept the compliment and feel good about it!

Love, although a wonderful feeling on its own, can be infused with fear; to love is to be vulnerable. Depending on the situation and relationship, love can lead to joy, fear or some combination of both. Similarly, joy can bring fear along with it. We might be afraid to lose the joy or the source of it, especially if it's a relational joy. Walking outside in the morning, feeling and smelling the newness of the day and basking in the wonderful feeling of being alive can be a great source of joy, as can many other 'stopping to smell the roses' moments. Since none of us walks around in a constant state of joy, it's important to grab those moments and appreciate them to the fullest! The same goes for feelings of love. We really need those good feeling moments as a counter-balance to the ones that don't feel so great.

I want to say more about feelings being free from judgment. I recall hearing former U.S. President Jimmy Carter confess that he had lusted in his heart. I understood what he meant and that he believed he had done wrong. I understand that he is not the only one to hold this belief. In reality, do our feelings make us bad, evil or even wrong? I contend they do not. It's so important that we learn to distinguish between feelings and behavior. If someone cuts us off in traffic, we might be so angry that we wish to retaliate. That's totally understandable, and we are completely blameless for feeling that. If, however, we have a gun and use it to shoot and kill the person who cut us off, we are guilty of murder. That is a behavior for which we are responsible and will receive severe negative consequences. This is a clear illustration of the difference between what we feel, as opposed to what we do. This ability to differentiate so often escapes people, that they judge their *feelings*. That judgment causes them to feel even worse about themselves, and it's my belief that they are suffering unnecessarily. Just because we are feeling something does not necessarily mean we have to act upon it. There are some circumstances when action is appropriate and even desirable. We always have choices about our behavior. If our emotions rule us beyond the point of rational choice, then something is amiss and worthy of attention and possibly of treatment.

Communication and Conflict Resolution

How *do* we resolve conflict? I like the term negotiate. Other choices include problem-solving, collaboration, and my least favorite, compromise, because I associate it with giving up something. For others, however, that association may not be there. In negotiation, both people speak up for what they want or need. They listen to what the other wants and needs, and then both look at options for resolution, which generally include some of what each of them wants or needs. If we are trying to decide on a restaurant, and I've been thinking about sushi all week, but you've been hankering for Italian food, we might decide on the basis of for whom it feels most compelling. Or we might flip a coin! We might choose Italian tonight and sushi the next time. There are many possibilities, and none necessitate an argument.

My belief, often stated is, "If one person wins, you both lose." No one is happy to lose. That unhappiness is bound to manifest in the other person. When we care about someone, we can't feel good about them losing. In addition, the 'loser' will probably have negative feelings quite likely resulting in resentment toward the 'winner.' The idea of a 'win/win' is so much better for both. Although it's human nature to feel a moment of triumph at a 'win,' this will pale by comparison to its cost.

Of course this example is about a trivial matter—what to eat for dinner. Although I see couples who say they're 'fighting' over the trivial all the time, it's never really about the trivial topic. It's the deeper issues, the feelings beneath, and the dynamic between them which are the real concerns. Although some concerns are more outwardly important, there is almost always a duality about the issue and what lies beneath. Rachel believes it is important that her children adhere to strict rules and have clear consequences if they don't. Her husband, Eric, who comes from a very different family of origin background, believes that once the rules are in place, the children have some say about consequences. Their son, Jeremy, a ninth grader, was not completing his homework. For Rachel, this would have necessitated removing all his privileges, electronics, 'screens,' grounding, withholding allowance, etc. For Eric, it required a conversation with Jeremy about the natural consequences (poor grades, potential failure of a class, etc.) He wanted their son to think about what would help him get his homework done and examine what was getting in the way. Somewhat begrudgingly, Rachel agreed to let Eric handle it, with the proviso that she be able to sign off on the outcome. After Eric's interaction with him, Jeremy was able to recognize that he wasn't particularly interested in the class he was potentially failing, and probably would benefit from tutoring, both from his teacher and if needed, from a private tutor. He was on board with a specific time slot for that particular class's homework with restrictions on screens, phone, etc. until he showed his parents his completed homework. When Rachel and Eric discussed his conversation with Jeremy, Rachel agreed to the plan, saying she thought it was a good one. It was not necessary for the couple to engage in an argument. Jeremy was a part of the solution, so he 'owned' it, was treated with respect about his opinions and options, and he learned not only conflict resolution but problem solving. It was definitely a 'win' for the three of them. It also taught Rachel that there are different paths other than the ones she learned in her family to arrive at a resolution. I believe it is imperative that children feel respected. Historically, this was not the case. Being respected is different from being in charge. Kids need adults to be in charge, no matter how much they protest otherwise. But all humans of all ages deserve and need to feel respected.

What constitutes a partnership? Sometimes, especially in romantic relationships, we have the belief we'll be so understood that the other will almost qualify as a mind reader—which obviously won't work. This is where the importance of communication comes in. The word 'communication' is bandied about all over the place. Many people think that they know what it is and that they know how to do it. If only it were that easy! And you might as well hear it now—no, 'If you loved me you'd know' doesn't hold any truth for couples, despite the fact that people often believe it does.

Pia Mellody gave her audience one of the most valuable tools I have ever come across on *Developing Personal Boundaries*. In a step-by-step 'how to talk and how to listen' presentation, she urges people to remember that they are speaking to be understood, and they are listening to understand. Many times people are so busy thinking about what they will say when the other pauses that they are not able to truly listen. Placing blame is not only nonproductive but creates a defensive response. Each of us is responsible for our own thoughts and our feelings. If we express ourselves from this vantage point the outcome is much, much better. This is not easy, since it's an almost complete about face of what we've always done. But it works, and what we've always done probably doesn't.

If you want the detailed description and explanation of just why and how this works, watch the referenced YouTube video. I highly recommend it—an hour well spent!

The speed at which Steve was driving caused Melissa a great deal of anxiety. They were vacationing in Colorado and traveling up to the mountains to a ski resort. Not only were the roads elevated, but they were winding as they ascended. He was having a wonderful time testing his mettle against the potentially perilous drive. Mindful of this, Melissa hated to rain on his parade, but when she could stand it no longer, she spoke up. She told him that she knew he was having fun; however she was imagining them plunging over the side of the winding road to meet their deaths in a fiery crash. She said that when she thought about that she felt extremely anxious and scared. She wondered if he'd mind slowing down or pulling over somewhere, so she could get herself into a less anxious state. Melissa took responsibility for her thoughts and feelings. Steve heard no blame since she never said he was doing something wrong. He could hear her fear and responded by saying he'd be happy to do either or both. How often does *that* happen? More typically, it goes something like this: "Are you crazy? Do you know how fast you're going? Do you know what would happen if you misjudged one curve?" And the defensive/offensive response: "I'm a perfectly capable driver, and I don't need you to backseat drive." At this point, no one would be happy. What's most important here is that in the interaction between Steve and Melissa, she was able to express her *fear*. Without blame, he had no need for defense and was open to hearing her feelings. In the second, more common example, he was blamed. He didn't hear her fear. He became defensive and shut her down. She did not make her need clear and therefore, did not get it met.

This is where 'I messages' come in handy, as does remembering not to blame. First, let me explain what an 'I message' is. It is simply speaking only about oneself, not another. We may say how we feel, what we think, what we want, how we disagree with someone else, and so on. It is easy to send a 'you' message disguised as an 'I' message. For example: "I feel really hurt when you act like such a baby."

Considering that most of us spent our childhoods trying to avoid blame, often tossing the blame ball to someone else, it's understandable that this is a difficult behavioral change to make. To create a good working partnership, blame needs to go away. That said, I recognize that people don't follow advice unless it's something they themselves want to do. I respect this greatly, as self-determination is what it's all about, and I'm not so deluded as to think I know what's best for everyone else.

Needs Vs Wants

Most of us get needs and wants confused or use them interchangeably. It's a safe bet that you're off track on the word 'need' in any sentence where that word is preceded by the word 'you,' i.e., "You need to take out the trash." First of all, it's very likely not a need for the other person. It's probably not even a need for you, but most likely a 'want,' and almost certainly yours, not necessarily his or hers. A more oblique manner of this occurs when someone says, "We need..." Again, it presumes to tell the other person what they 'need.'

Some examples of differentiating between wants and needs would include: I want an ice cream cone. I need a warmer coat. I need you to hear me. I want you to come with me to the store. As we become more aware of differentiating, we become more easily able to discern the difference and decide in which category we want or need to place those words.

I return to Abraham Maslow for delineating our needs and their place in the hierarchy of importance. In his original hierarchy of needs, he listed five basic human needs: biological and physiological, safety, love, esteem and self-actualization.

Maslow developed this in the 1940s. Changes were made to the original model by him and others in the 1970s and 1980s to include cognitive, aesthetic, and transcendence needs.

The more we identify our needs, the better our chances for getting them met, providing we are able to express them appropriately and depending upon the capability of others to meet those needs. Wants count as being important as well. We have the right to our wants alongside with our needs. We have the right to give them expression.

John Gray, author of *Men Are From Mars, Women Are From Venus*, states that the primary needs of women and men are different. This doesn't mean we don't all have the same needs. It's a matter of priority. He says that for men, the three primary needs are: acceptance (for who they are); appreciation (for what they do), and trust (for their competence and instinct to protect.) The primary needs are referenced from John, but what's in the parentheses is my interpretation of what they mean. For women, he describes the following three primary needs: to feel cared about, to be understood, and to be respected. I believe women might especially need respect as we so lacked it historically, which takes nothing away from the obvious fact that men need it as well. It's important to recognize individual variations as well as gender differences. We want to give others what they need, as opposed to assuming that what they need is the same as what we need and operating from that assumption.

In addition to presumed gender differences, there are differences in how we experience feeling loved and cared about. Many of my clients have found Gary Chapman's *The Five Love Languages: The Secret to Love that Lasts* to be extremely helpful in their relationships and communication. We often give what *we* want or need, so we may be giving someone important to us something they don't want or need with the very best of intentions. Discovering which 'love language' we each speak in is a tremendous help in facilitating both good communication and mutual satisfaction in a relationship. We may have several 'love languages', but most have one or two primary ones. To explain how this works, if my primary language is 'acts of service' and yours is 'touch,' I may expect you to feel loved by acts of service, without realizing that doesn't 'speak' to you the way touch does. It may seem simple, but discerning your own and determining the other's require effort, and the benefits are well worth it.

Feelings Vs Thoughts

Another frequent misuse of language is the often heard "I feel" when what we're really talking about is what we think. Some examples: "I feel like you always have to get your way," "I feel like you're trying to make this about you." We don't realize we're not actually stating a feeling. For effective communication, clarifying the difference between a feeling and a thought is as important as clarifying the difference between a want and a need. Often when we speak we're not really thinking about the actual meaning of the words we use, but rather using expressions with which we're familiar. In these examples, the use of "I feel" can be a way of disguising a 'You message' containing blame. It's often not a conscious thought. Speaking of blame, it's not my intention to find fault with the misuse of words. Instead I want to encourage people to work toward clarity of thought about what they are saying. I believe that making these distinctions helps provide a path toward enabling good communication, despite how much initial work it may take to achieve. With practice, it becomes easier.

If the takeaway from this section is nothing more, I sincerely hope it will be to once again underscore the importance of adding the 'You' without sacrificing the 'Me.' As we move to romantic partnerships, it becomes even clearer why establishing and maintaining this stance is essential.

● ● ●

"The glory of friendship is not the outstretched hand, not the kindly smile, nor the joy of companionship; it is the spiritual inspiration that comes to one when you discover that someone else believes in you and is willing to trust you with a friendship."

—*Ralph Waldo Emerson*

Part Three

Now Us

"We're all a little weird. And life is a little weird. And when we find someone whose weirdness is compatible with ours, we join up with them and fall into mutually satisfying weirdness—and call it love— true love."

— *Robert Fulghum*

We looked at First Me, Then You, so the next natural progression would be 'Us.' 'Us' constitutes a committed romantic relationship between two people. Again, for simplicity's sake, I will continue to use a heterosexual model. The same 'rules' apply to most couples, whatever their gender. While I will make some broad generalizations about gender differences in an effort to clarify and better understand the opposite gender, these are intended to be helpful, despite the inevitable exceptions. Nowhere has the subject of gender differences been more humorously and intelligently illustrated than in Rob Becker's one man play, *Defending the Caveman*. Rob is both brilliant and humble, in addition to being one of the funniest people I've had the pleasure to know. (I had the privilege of interviewing him for a radio show I previously hosted.) I wish there were a full version of it for all couples to see. However, there are some clips online showing parts of his show. I recommended it to all the couples I saw while Rob was still performing. There are some partial renditions by other actors on YouTube, but the flavor isn't quite the same. The cherry on top is the fact that Rob found a way to gently poke fun at both genders, while never treating anyone disrespectfully. That is no small feat.

People are sometimes surprised to learn that many issues of same gender couples bear a striking resemblance to hetero couples. I believe it boils down to a few things. One, each one of us is unique. So, put two unique people together, and you're bound to get 'issues.' Two, we all struggle with similar complexities such as communication, trust, boundaries, etc. Three, we all assume roles in our relationships. The pros and cons of those roles will out, no matter the gender.

Clearly, relationships provide a challenge. The high divorce rate tells us that—just in case we hadn't noticed! People often muse about the still married and wonder how many of those are happily so. I do believe in and have seen good and healthy marriages. I've also seen people locked in unhappy relationships who remain stuck for a multitude of reasons, quite often not the ones they might tell you or themselves about. That's usually because they don't know; it's unconscious. Wouldn't it be interesting if we could get an honest and true accounting of how many people are happily married and, in addition, how many happily married people are married to equally happily married spouses?

● ● ●

Keeping the Me in the Us

What it Means to be a Couple

Perhaps the most difficult challenge we face as couples is just this: how do we come together so closely, yet still be able to separate and be whole on our own? An often used phrase in movies, TV and real life, "You complete me," might be the mantra for co-dependency. I've got a metaphor I like for this one, which both illustrates the point and stimulates the appetite! Our goal is to be a fully baked 'cake.' When we form a relationship with a significant other, we get the icing. Cake without icing is a good and tasty treat. Icing enhances the taste and adds something rich to the cake, but the cake can stand alone, leaving us complete. When both cakes are 'iced' by their union with each other, something extra special is added.

Some couples believe that to be a couple is to be joined at the hip. Other couples are ships passing in the night. Optimum connection entails being together and sharing things as a couple, as well as having one's own individual interests, pursuits, relationships, etc. Fairy tales inform us that when we find 'true love' we will not only be living happily ever after, but basically living as one entity.

In *Mating in Captivity*, Esther Perel states that it is the space between the couple that leaves room for eroticism. She contends that a basic dilemma in long term relationships is the juxtaposition of security versus eroticism. Since we are attempting to have both, it can be very challenging to find the right combination. She also refers to the erotic space between a couple as the place where uncertainty and mystery are contained. This same uncertainty and mystery is a large part of the erotic connection early in a relationship. Once security is attained, it may well be at the sacrifice of erotic intimacy. Balancing these two is essential for a healthy and happy long-term relationship.

Another metaphor, borrowed from my editor, Tuesday Thomson, is:

> Alone I am a complete circle. I never sought my 'better half' because I am a complete whole on my own. Instead, I sought other circles, trying to avoid people who saw themselves as half circles. In uniting with another complete whole, we created a new object, in a third dimension. When two circles intersect, mathematically they create a sphere. They both remain circles independent of one another, but together they create something more than they could ever be on their own.

The cover of this book represents this as the 'o' in 'Loving.' It is the two circles intersecting into a sphere. As Tuesday noted, this is probably a good metaphor for men—my weak spot—probably in part because it is mathematical, another area in which I can always use help! So my many thanks and kudos to Tuesday, not only for the wonderful concept, but for its important presence on the front of this book.

As opposed to the 'whole,' there is the 'hole.' This is the one people believe their partner will fill, but sadly, this doesn't work. Although we may complement each other, we can't fill the holes to complete the other. This can only be accomplished by ourselves. After all, when we fall in love, don't we pretty much think that person is the best thing since sliced bread? Imagine falling in love with yourself and feeling that great about *your* self! Only then will we truly believe someone else could love us, for we will know ourselves to be loveable. It is sad to see how often people don't possess this love and appreciation for themselves, and how frequently their partner tries to love them enough to convince them they are loveable. If you've tried it, you know it won't do the trick. Intuitively, it makes sense. To the extent that we have learned to love ourselves, we can measure the likelihood of a healthy, successful relationship.

Osi Mizrahi's article in The Huffington Post, *The Search for Intimacy.* 'In-to-me-see' speaks to this concept. She states that for there to be real intimacy, a person must truly know, understand and love themselves. She suggests that before asking the question, "Do I have the right partner?" you should first ask the question, "Am I a person I would want to be with?" If the answer is 'Yes,' then you are in a very good position to find the person you want to be with and create a loving partnership. Mizrahi speaks to the notion of loving oneself as including enjoying your own company and being a good friend to yourself. She goes on to say that we attract what we are. If you buy the premise, not only does loving yourself benefit you, it also paves the way to finding the right person for you. I'd call that a definite win/win!

I can't stress enough the importance of this. The theme of being completed by another and the subsequent reinforcement in our culture can lead us down a treacherous path. I say this because it promotes the absence of a self in the context of a relationship. Long ago, the 'urge to merge' became a common expression regarding people's desire to have a partner. We do have this urge, and it's a good thing. Aside from what it can bring to us as individuals, it's the cornerstone of families and perpetuation of the species. Problems arise when we are unable to separate again after the merger. The process of coming together and coming apart is a dance, a metaphor I first heard used many years ago by Harriet

Lerner, first in *The Dance of Anger*, and in her subsequent 'Dance' books. In *The Dance of Intimacy,* Lerner offers wonderful illustrations of relationship dynamics. If, in the intimacy dance, we become stuck together, we lose ourselves, (and as Lerner puts it, we are 'de-selfed.') We are static. If we become too distant, we lose the connection, as well as the dance between us. It is this movement toward and away from one's partner that is the dance itself. Being devoid of either a sense of self or a sense of intimacy is a great loss. In a healthy relationship we require both.

Much has been studied and written in the field of marriage and family therapy about what is called "The Distancer/Pursuer Pattern." Dr. John Gottman, professor emeritus in psychology at the University of Washington, who is considered a leading expert in the field of couple's therapy noted that this destructive pattern is a common cause of divorce if not resolved. This subscribes to the theory that it is a personality trait; however, I have seen couples for whom this behavior is more relational than personality based. Lerner also addresses this dynamic and describes the pattern as,

> "A partner with pursuing behavior tends to respond to relationship stress by moving *toward* the other. They seek communication, discussion, togetherness and expression. This person is anxious, urgent and often critical of their partner for being emotionally unavailable. A partner with distancing behavior tends to respond to relationship stress by moving *away* from the other. They want physical and emotional distance. They have difficulty with vulnerability."

The pursuing partner is labeled demanding and feels disconnected in the *manner* they need to feel connected. The distancing partner is labeled unavailable and feels pressured by the pursuit. As is apparent, this is not a good pattern in which to remain. Although I've seen couples stuck in this mode, I've also witnessed a turnabout when the pursuer can stop chasing long enough (and it might take a while) for the distancer to notice the conspicuous absence and seek to remedy it by becoming the pursuer. In a healthy relationship, taking turns in this way creates a certain symmetry in this interchange, which, on balance, can work well for the couple. When the couple is stuck, the symmetry has vanished, and something has gone awry.

A friend once described her need for connection as being like a plant requiring watering. I've always liked that simile. One way or another, I believe it applies to all of us, whatever the nature and frequency of our individual 'watering' needs may be. Going back to the original "Me do it," our need for autonomy must also be fulfilled by us and respected by our partner.

* * *

Communication

We seem to think that communication should be simple; however, it is far from that. When I was a kid, we had a game we called 'telephone.' Everyone sat in a circle and one person started by whispering something into the ear of the person sitting next to them. The whispers continued around the circle until they reached the last person before the original speaker. That last person would tell everyone in the circle what they heard. It never even came close to matching what the first person had said. No matter how small the circle, this would always be true. Often, the results provoked laughter. What we say and what someone else hears often do not match. This has vast implications in life, and especially for a couple.

As challenging as this may be, there are ways to improve upon our communications. First are the 'I messages' I referenced earlier. Taking responsibility for your thoughts and feelings without blaming the other is the goal. If we are going to reference another in an 'I' message, it is very important that we reference something that is not subjective and certainly not insulting! If it is subjective, it's best to state it in that way. An example of this would be, "When you didn't answer when I spoke to you, I thought you were ignoring me. I'm not sure that's true, however." One I often use to illustrate this is, "When you don't call to let me know you're going to be late, I feel hurt and question my importance to you." In both examples, the other person is given an opportunity to explain, if the perception does not match their intent. Understanding how their behavior impacts the other reduces defensiveness. Defense very rarely leads to a positive outcome, unless it is more an explanation than a defense and includes an acknowledgment of the other person's feelings, even if their perceptions do not match. Once again, this is an important area in which to keep boundaries intact.

Next is something called 'reflective listening.' Despite the fact that many couples find this a tedious exercise, it is a very effective tool for finding out if the message we sent was the one received, and if the message we heard was actually sent. Generally this works well if the person being spoken to says something like, "I heard you say, 'fill-in-the-blank.'" The original speaker can say that the other person heard them accurately, can modify some of what was heard, or can say, "That wasn't what I meant, so let me try again." Think about what it feels like when someone tells you that you're not understanding what they meant. There is blame implicit in that statement. Far better to take responsibility for your own communication and simply say, "I'm not sure that I said that clearly, so I'll express it differently." In essence, you are taking a one down position, which can be a very helpful stance to maintain. It is the polar opposite of one-upsmanship, which is almost always guaranteed to end badly. You might secretly think they didn't understand you, but telling them that is never helpful. That brings me back to a favorite adage, "Would you rather be right or effective?"

In her You Tube talk on boundaries, Pia Mellody weaves together the concepts of boundaries: listening to understand the other person, talking to be understood—not to control or manipulate, not placing blame and not taking blame that doesn't belong to us, taking responsibility for our own thoughts and feelings, and negotiating solutions to disagreements. She indicates that if we feel blamed, we become defensive. As Gottman has stated, defensiveness is a toxic element in a relationship. What he refers to as criticism (another toxic element) is a first cousin to blame. Yet blame and defensiveness are so often an automatic way of relating, it takes a great deal of awareness and effort to stop both. Explanation is different from defense or justification. If we can step back far enough to consciously hear ourselves before we speak, we are capable of making this distinction. In mental health terms, it is known as developing an 'observing ego.' Some examples of justification include, "I only did that because you did it first." and "I wouldn't have done it if you hadn't (fill in the blank)." It's a way of saying we're not guilty or even responsible for our deeds because of what someone else did or failed to do. That's not taking ownership of ourselves and our own behavior, and it won't ever get us anywhere we really want to go. Defensiveness is similar, but not identical. "That's not what I said." "It isn't my fault." "You only say that to make me feel guilty," are some examples.

How does explanation differ from those? Let's look at how it works with Adam and Aubrey. Aubrey has to work late, and Adam has arrived home from his job before her and started to cook dinner. Aubrey is an attorney, and she is working on a case going to trial in the morning. She feels pressured and is soon completely absorbed in getting her work finished. She totally forgets to call Adam to let him know she'll be late. In the meantime, Adam has finished cooking, tried texting Aubrey (her phone is in her office, and she's working in the conference room, so she doesn't hear it) and is beginning to wonder if he should be worried or angry. It's not like her to leave him in the dark, so he begins to think of all the bad things that might have happened to her. As time passes, he decides to go ahead and eat without her, as he's hungry, and not so sure he should be worried instead of angry. Just about the time Adam finishes his meal, Aubrey stands up to stretch and realizes how late it is. She starts to reach for her phone, realizes it's not there and goes back into her office to find Adam's text. She immediately calls him and tells him that she lost track of time and how sorry she is.

He says he was worried, but also angry because he made dinner, which is now cold. She acknowledges her understanding of his feelings, is sorry he was worried and also sorry he went to the trouble of making dinner for her, and she didn't show up to eat it. She doesn't go into details about what she was doing, why she lost track of time, how pressured she feels or in any way justify her actions. She hears him, accepts responsibility for causing him worry and anger and apologizes to him. She asks if there's anything she can do to make it up to him—perhaps pick up some dessert on the way home. Adam is relieved she's okay, feels heard and appreciates her apology and effort to make things better. He says no thanks to dessert, asks when he can expect her home and both leave the conversation feeling resolved.

That's not how it usually goes. Aubrey didn't justify herself or defend herself. Had she done either of those, the chances are good that things might have escalated between them, and an argument might have ensued. She didn't make it about her, just listened, cared and responded to what Adam was telling her. It sounds so simple when I say it here. We all know that in real life, it's not that easy. But it *is* effective!

Another suggestion about using our wise minds is to remind ourselves we don't have to have an immediate response to everything anyone says. We can pause, ponder and answer slowly in the moment. Or, we can take a time out and tell them we want to think about our answer and will get back to them when we have it. The important thing with the last is that we must honor our word and follow through at a later time. Oftentimes people don't say something because of fear the listener will interpret it incorrectly. Why not just admit that fear before saying what they want to say? An example would be, "I'm worried this will sound blaming, but that's not what I intend, so please let me know if you hear it that way." Better to qualify than to omit, in my opinion. If we couple our feelings with our wise minds to determine our behavior, we are capable of finding ways of expression which foster a positive outcome rather than a negative one.

Disagreements

Boundaries, communication, the Four Agreements, three questions and many other factors play an important role and help determine a positive outcome for disagreements between a couple. Yet competition (who has suffered the most, been the most unjustly and unfairly treated, who is the guiltiest, who started it, etc.) and the incessant need to be 'right' dominate most couples' relationships. When people tell me they are arguing over 'the little things' or 'silly things,' I suggest that they are not arguing over the trivial, but over the profound—something much bigger and more important than the actual topic of conversation. Often they experience feeling hurt, unimportant, unjustly accused, not a priority, ignored, not understood, etc., which comprise the underlying reason(s) for the disagreement. As far as arguments, they are to be reserved for judicial courts and debate teams. Instead, disagreements are what couples will ideally be having, and just forget about fights. Those only belong in the ring. In having this discourse, it is always a challenge for me to avoid the 'should' word, one we all tend to use a great deal. Whoever said, "Don't should on yourself," is to be commended for establishing a baseline. I sometimes have to work hard to avoid that word!

Often our parents are our models for being a couple. Whether we are taught by example what to do or what to avoid, we may be hampered by our perception of what is true. We don't know what goes on behind closed doors. I frequently hear, "My parents never argued," and although it's possibly true, it's more likely that it was out of earshot of their kids. If they truly never argued, there was most likely a lot of 'going along to get along' on one or both parts. If the parents argued, it was most likely done in a manner which wasn't healthy, e.g. combative, competitive, disrespectful. If our parents are affectionate, we see that as the norm. If they never touch each other and maintain distance physically, that becomes our standard. If parents talk to their children about their spouse in negative ways or utter the mandate, "Don't tell your father/mother," we see a model for a lack of loyalty and honesty. And so it goes.

Those who grow up never seeing their parents disagree, and believe and assume that their parents never 'fought' are at a distinct disadvantage. As a result, when they are in a relationship, they think there is something terribly wrong because they have disagreements and conflict. The belief the child held might not be accurate and is definitely not a healthy or realistic expectation. In the absence of conflict, there is no opportunity to learn conflict resolution and to learn to express anger in a healthy manner. Does anyone *ever* teach us how to express anger appropriately or resolve conflict in a healthy manner? How frequently are we taught how to work collaboratively rather than competitively with a partner? The answer is quite simply either never or hardly ever. Thus, we are sorely lacking a skill set enabling us to have a healthy and close relationship with another human being. This model of no disagreements can be as much a detriment as seeing parents arguing all the time. Neither portrays a healthy relationship.

There is something that commonly occurs in relationships called 'sweeping it under the rug.' People tell themselves things like, "It isn't that important; I need to just get over this; I don't want to start a fight," etc. Whatever gets swept under the rug builds in height to the point that people start tripping over it. That's when the real trouble begins. Sweeping it under the rug no longer works. Not only are they tripping, they are pretty much up to here.

In a recent *Psychology Today* article written by Kristin Ohlson, *The Einstein of Love*, couples expert John Gottman has taken a very different position than the one most people and many marriage therapists embrace, and I agree with him. Concerning the idea that brushing off the small stuff (i.e. pick your battles) is a good thing, Gottman says: "Wrong. The best relationship is one in which partners not only actively repair regrettable incidents—but do so quickly." His "Threshold of Repair" metric demonstrates that partners who acknowledge their attacks and immediately reach out to make amends keep a trivial hurt from growing into a progressively larger one in which negativity compounds rapidly.

The topics of disagreement span a wide array. Some common areas of conflict are: money and who, how and on what to spend or save it, shared responsibility, families of origin, jealousy, and envy. Sometimes digging deep allows people to find the 'root' cause of a problem and to solve it, as well.

This was the case with Luke and Jessica. I recall repeatedly hearing Luke's lament about how Jessica never put his needs before hers, yet he was always doing so for her. After many attempts to uncover the source, Luke finally acknowledged that he envied Jessica's ability to feel good enough about herself to give herself what she needed. Whereas he—because he was so determined to be a 'nice' guy who never truly believed in his worthiness—hadn't developed the ability to do this. His envy for this quality kept him angry at Jessica and feeling unimportant to her, which did nothing to help his sense of worth. In addition to his inability to give himself what he needed and deserved, he was determined to prove that he was doing it the 'right' way. He couldn't open his mind to the possibility that she might actually be a good role model for him. Jessica had never made the connection between her own healthy self-care and Luke's lower levels of self-esteem as a cause for criticism. After finally learning this, she could understand the reason behind their continuing pattern of conflict. Instead of seeing him as uncaring, selfish and lacking in sensitivity, she could at last see his struggle and better support him in working toward growth.

When it comes to money, it's often a matter of communication and agreement. Charles was an avid athlete who spent money on workout clothes, gym memberships and sporting events. Cheryl, his wife, was into magazines in a big way. She loved to subscribe to quite a few and devoured them when they arrived in the mail. Charles and Cheryl thought that each other's interests were superficial and unimportant, and both believed the other was simply wasting money. When I suggested that both give up what they so enjoyed in order to restore equilibrium to the relationship, they were able to unite against my preposterous suggestion. They finally understood that it would be a deprivation for both, no matter their different priorities. Just because it wasn't important to one didn't mean it wasn't to the other. Where they had shared interests, money was not an issue. In fact, money was not really the issue at all. The more complex aspects of their relationship, such as trust, fear and control, were being enacted around money and hobbies. As they understood and accepted their differences they became less likely to form negative judgments and more likely to trust their ability to communicate more effectively to hear and be heard.

Prioritizing the New Family

One of the most common areas of conflict in a couple's relationship occurs when one partner feels they come after the original family of their partner. A classic example, and a fairly typical one, was presented by Ryan and Kelly. Ryan's mom pretty much thought he hung the moon. Kelly was more objective about Ryan, so he always felt better getting Mom's version of the truth. Often, Kelly felt she was left to fend for herself, as well as for their children, if Mom wanted something. She was unable to tell Ryan this in a manner he could hear. They kept having the same argument over and over. For Ryan, it was a blind spot; for Kelly, it was emblazoned in neon lights. Finally, after enough time and discussion in therapy, Ryan came to see that he had neglected to prioritize his 'now' family instead of his original family. He made the shift and was open to hearing from Kelly when she experienced feeling displaced. Once again, I can't emphasize the importance of this enough. People will usually say they want to come first—before the original family and to know their partners have their backs. I would say the partner comes second (to yourself), and thus becomes the primary 'you,' as opposed to mom, dad, siblings, etc. Does this mean we stop caring about our original families? No, not at all. We can remain close to our loved ones as long as we pay attention to how our partners experience us. We decide what it looks like to take care of ourselves first, our partners second, and the rest (including children) third—with exceptions made when appropriate.

● ● ●

Gender Roles

Are the Times 'A-changing?'

As a 'baby boomer,' I was raised in the 1950s and 1960s, so I began my life with a stay at home mom, breadwinner dad, and the old traditional couple's roles so well depicted on television by shows such as *Make Room for Daddy* and *Father Knows Best.* Although these were good shows, they depicted the historical stereotypical gender roles. Then along came the Women's Movement, and all that "a woman's place is in the home" stuff got thrown out in favor of Carly Simon daring to question the merit of marriage in *That's the Way I've Always Heard It Should Be*, and we were off and running. What to do? Should I listen to my mom and all my childhood teachings or discard them and become a women's libber with all the rights and freedoms embodied therein? Like many of my generation, I probably am a composite of both. The longer I live, the more I experience, I continue learning how to find my own path and what works best for me.

Our adult children also comprise a composite. Raised by my generation, they were subjected to many of our mixed messages, and our children's children have gotten a watered down version of that. In many ways, they are freed. Others are confounded by too many options. So often, motherhood equates with guilt. As with my generation, the dual desire of motherhood and career (when both are there) present an open door policy. But if we don't want to work outside the home, we may feel guilty for not contributing income. If we *do* want a career or just to interact with adults during the days (and, I might add, be able to visit a restroom all by ourselves!), we will feel guilty about leaving our children in the care of others. The book, *Perfect Madness: Motherhood in the Age of Anxiety* written by Judith Warner, spells it out well. As with most things in this gray world we inhabit, there is no right or wrong. Sometimes we long for black and white where the answers are clear and we have no choices to make, but then our freedom becomes limited. No easy solutions.

I'd be remiss if I didn't address the subject of connection. Today's world is unique in its vast iterations of the word. Yet, we are so connected that we seem to disconnect more and more. I was so struck by the television commercial that displayed a line of young people facing the camera all lost in their phones and not interacting at all with each other. I've even found myself and my kids sitting side by side and playing Words with Friends on our phones instead of pulling out the good old Scrabble board (which we used often in their growing up years) and actually interacting while we were together! Hence, the more connected...

Then we have 'texting.' This is actually a new word in our vocabulary and apparently our dictionaries. The word 'text' existed, of course, however it is a noun, whereas 'texting' is a verb. Now the word 'text' is also at times a verb, as in, "Don't text and drive." It even has a past tense—'texted,' as in, "I texted her about our meeting." Although the Internet has opened up so much opportunity in so many ways, it generally represents a method of communication fraught with misunderstanding potential. Tone of voice, inflection, etc. are all lost due to the lack of verbal exchange. Sometimes it is more effective to write than to speak. For example, I'm writing a book, not delivering a speech. I will confess that the absence of emoticons or at least a colon followed by parentheses has proven to be challenging when I want to impart that something is tongue-in-cheek or meant to be humorous.

Despite the fact that we are so almost constantly connected by various 'screens,' we seem to be less emotionally and even physically connected than ever before. As one person put it, "These touch screens are keeping us out of touch." Although many people seem unaware of this, I believe people are becoming increasingly attuned to this absence of real connection. In fact, that this is something deeply felt by many is attested to by the YouTube video, *Look Up* by Gary Turk, which has had over 56,834,678 views as of this writing. It poetically illuminates the disconnection that occurs between people when we bury ourselves in our digital devices.

Although the Internet connects us, as does texting in its own way, I maintain that using our words verbally and directing them toward someone who can actually hear them as they are spoken is a far more effective method of communication. By the way, (and how difficult not to just write 'BTW'), I'm not including 'tweets' and all the other modes of connection, although I'm aware they exist! To include all social media, I might have to write a second book. And, let's not forget about speaking on the phone, which still comes in second to in-person communication because it's missing all the visual cues.

Let's look at this in the context of the couple. Someone mentioned an article in an unknown (to me) issue of *Psychology Today* magazine addressing the issue of couples' losing their connection by virtue of connection to devices. From what I observe and what I hear from others, it hit home for many. How often do we automatically check a text or other message in the midst of conversation, dinner, and amazingly, even at a funeral, without giving a thought to the fact that it is actually impolite and dismissive behavior? Since the interruption didn't start with us but with the phone, we don't consider that we are actually interrupting by turning our attention elsewhere. But, indeed, we are! So often people tell me they wish they'd had the tools to make relationships work long before they came to see me. Perhaps this might constitute such a tool. Give the person you're talking with your full attention!

One of Becker's Caveman stories involves the 'chip bowl.' He maintains that if a bunch of guys are sitting around eating chips and the bowl becomes empty it will go like this: "I brought the chips." "I ate the chips." "I brought the bowl." and "It's my house." Finally, the excuses run out, and whoever is left without one has to get the bowl refilled. This is clearly a competition, and it has a loser—the guy who has to refill the bowl. Becker describes a very different scenario for women. He says that if the chip bowl is empty, all the women get up, go into the kitchen together, and the bowl is refilled. This is clearly a collaboration without a winner or a loser. Although this is a generalization on both counts, (women are capable of being competitive and men of being collaborative) it speaks to an important gender or perhaps a socialization difference.

While many little girls are playing with dolls and playing house, little boys are finding ways to compete, whether with toys, video games, sports or whatever might be handy. This in in part our nature and in part how we are nurtured. So when a woman asks a man to help with housework or childcare and is met with resistance, her perception is that he doesn't want to help her. Do I even need to say how damaging this is to both? He's not saying he doesn't care about her wants and needs; he's merely operating from a different perspective. Once a man can see and appreciate this, he is almost always willing (and sometimes even happy) to share the responsibility. But we women are often guilty of expecting men to be like us and taking it personally or as a sign of something being wrong with them if they are not like us. That's not to say that men don't do this as well. Of course there are always exceptions to the rule, and I'm generalizing again, but there really are gender differences. It has actually been discovered that parts of women's and men's brains are different. The connection between right and left brain is stronger in women, and the parts of the brain which control depth perception and night vision are stronger in men. In my humble opinion, you can often track it all back to cave times, despite the stereotyping, and I do think Becker had the right idea—at least as it may apply today. One last example of this is why (many) men don't want to ask for directions. In cave times, men were hunting for food; now they are hunting for destinations. No 'traditional' cave guy would have been able to hold his head up if he asked another guy, "Where is the food?" And women, the gatherers, had to be able to look around for the provisions they needed to complete the family's needs. Left brain to right brain, or as we like to call it, 'multi-tasking.'

Mythology

Beginning in childhood our lives are populated by many myths and fantasies, especially about the opposite sex. For starters, we have "Guys only want one thing." I could, and often do, go on about that one. Gentlemen, let me be clear that although I've raised two sons, I never pretend to know as much about the male gender as I do the female one. So feel free to tell me if I get any of this wrong! However, there is a time in a young man's life, when he is infused by hormones which rule his thoughts about sex.

Yet even then girls do not cease to be people and worth caring about. But, that one-dimensional sex myth is so damaging, I wish there were a way to extinguish its power entirely. It's definitely a chicken and egg thing when our culture portrays this mythology as 'truth in advertising' in all forms of media, etc. I know 'sex sells,' but that is a very different concept and applies to women, as well as men. I'm betting more women bought *Fifty Shades of Grey* than men! On the other hand, part of that book could be a learning experience for men about what many women want in bed, e.g. a slow hand and prolonged foreplay to create eager desire. I've actually heard that many men decided to read it to find out why their partners did. But, back to the myth; let's take it apart to understand why it is toxic.

If guys only want one thing, they are something less than human- sex machines if you will. Sex is a disembodied concept which has no attachment to a person whatsoever. Similarly, women are something less than human as well—objects of desire that must possess the requisite charms, body and sex appeal to attract the man who only wants one thing. But then there's the female conundrum: women who enjoy sex are 'sluts' and women who don't enjoy sex are 'frigid.' If ever there was a no-win situation, that's it. In these scenarios, both genders are devalued, and rendered less than human. Men are oftentimes surprised that many women continue to believe this myth forever. For women, it becomes a belief about their own value, as well as a mechanism by which to reduce men to a simple and unflattering cliché. For men it is a painful entrapment, again saying something negative about their own value and the value they place upon women. Suffice it to say, I really dislike this myth and its perpetuation of a very negative stereotype.

Toward the goal of changing the myth, I highly recommend an article written by Alyssa Royse on goodmenproject.com entitled *'The Danger in Demonizing Male Sexuality.'* She does an excellent job of not only defining the mythology but giving suggestions for changing it, including things such as recommending that men ask women what they want, that men let women in instead of luring them in, and don't take it personally if the answer is 'no.' Women then have the opportunity to believe that consensual sex is a good and pleasurable experience for both, without judgment being rendered as to the man's motives. This eliminates a woman's fear that he sees her as an object. And ladies, you'll have to speak up for this to work.

Before I move forward, a caveat: there are some men who are so obsessed with sex that it drives them to seek it out at almost any cost. I want to state emphatically that this is not typical of most men. There are men who are obsessed with other things, as well, just as there are women who are obsessed with sex and with other things. Obsessions abound, whether they be related to sex, food, pack ratting, cleanliness, etc. They are so common that it has become popular to refer to someone as 'OCD.' For the record, that actually refers to a diagnosis known as Obsessive Compulsive Disorder. Thus, if we're going to insist upon pinning a diagnosis on someone or use a descriptive term, 'OC' would actually be more accurate, as it stands for obsessive compulsive. In other words, you can't 'be' a disorder!

Let's look at the female counterpart to guys only want one thing: 'Women use sex for power and control.' Have males ever mindlessly pursued sex for the sake of sex? Have women ever used sex for power and/or control? Absolutely. But, and here's the important part: women, as a rule, do not use sex in this way. The myth is created by several factors. Historically women were disempowered in almost every aspect of their lives. To the extent that they felt they could claim ownership over their own bodies, they might refuse sex and be reasonably certain that a refusal wouldn't result in rape. To a man, this might very well seem controlling, especially if he is being denied the sexual intimacy he seeks. Women are the gatekeepers of sex. They consent or fail to consent to participate in sexual activities and generally need emotional connection to precede sexual intimacy. Many men require both, as well. What so many couples miss is one of the truest things I've ever heard about sexual intimacy: "Foreplay begins when you get up in the morning." What that means is that everything that transpires between couples in a relationship can pave the way to sexual intimacy or establish impassible roadblocks to it. So often, people are ignorant of this very important fact. For example, if a woman feels unimportant, undesirable, disrespected, burdened, taken for granted, or anything else negative coming from her partner, she will most likely have no interest in sex. Partners are often astonished to see a rekindling of desire when a sufficient interest in them and their needs is shown. Here's an important note that often surprises women—this is often the same for men, as well. Why are women surprised? Because, after all, 'Guys only want one thing!'

Ironically, the truth is that many women actually give up their power regarding sexuality when they are in a committed relationship. She will usually feel she must at least maintain whatever sexual practices with her partner which have already been established. What most men don't realize is that women fear being judged by men. This may lead to some very negative consequences, which I will address in the section about sex.

The partner who is disinclined to be sexual for whatever reason, oftentimes feels guilty as well as resentful. The partner who is interested in sexual intimacy feels rejected, resentful, and disconnected. Then, there is the problem of not being able to talk about it. Eventually they either resign themselves to the status quo, seek out help from someone like myself, find another sexual partner, or part ways. Clearly there's a great deal of sexual mythology in our perceptions of the opposite gender which does not further the cause of successful and happy relationships.

Other myths include 'If you loved me you'd know,' and its twin 'I already told you, so if you cared, you'd remember.' One double-edged sword of long term relationships is that we get to know our partner, a positive, but we presume to know their minds better than they, which is not so positive. Of course, we could have some awareness our partner doesn't see, but the final authority must rest with the person who tells his or her truth as they see it. We are all capable of using glittering generalities—always, never, ever, etc. I see this more frequently with women, and hope we can all learn to 'Never say never.' It might feel like never, but seldom is that an accurate description of a fact. Kristen and Mark were quite adept in the area of assumptions. I often heard one or both of them say things like, "I know what you're thinking," "I know what you're going to say," or "I know what that look means." This not only took mind reading to the nth degree, but it effectively cut off communication and oftentimes created resentment. If we had the ability to read someone's mind, it would be not only amazing, but would clearly eliminate the need to communicate! I've seen many an argument on this very topic, and it would be amusing if it weren't so painful. It reminds me of the joke about the cheating spouse who, caught in the act, says, "Who are you going to believe—me or your lying eyes?"

My experience has allowed me to come to some theories about the power struggle that often exists with a couple. What women usually fail to note is the vital fact that all men started out as some 'mommy's' little boy. The power differential was huge in favor of Mom. Just because they grow up (usually to be taller and bigger than us), doesn't make females any less powerful than that first woman in their lives. This is a tremendous blind spot for both women and men. Similarly, the father was bigger, had a booming voice and for a girl was her first 'man.' Often, in the past especially, these men were not frequently present, and a great amount of insecurity arose for both genders about their fathers being unattainable. But for women, it is somewhat different, and it transfers onto their adult male partners. They often see the man as the more powerful and themselves as questing after his often elusive love and approval, once again, revisiting the experience of childhood and Dad. So if both see themselves as less powerful (if you buy the theory), then it's no wonder the tug of war for power exists.

When I work with a couple, and they tell me things are better between them, I ask them what changed. More times than not, they point to the other person, and that's how they see it. Owning one's power and truly seeing the vulnerability of our partner is an often difficult yet an essential step toward understanding our power to effect someone we love while wielding it wisely and kindly. If we liken it to how we see our power in relation to children, it can help open our eyes. Until we recognize our ability to impact the other, we might just keep on flailing out, never realizing the damage being inflicted. It's really not David and Goliath at all. It's just 'us,' and we're both sitting in the same leaky canoe.

Another myth I often hear from men is that men are just simple. Women, they tell me, are complex. They're not wrong about the women; however, I doubt any woman would describe men as simple! Or, if they would, they would probably say they couldn't understand men—simple or not.

One last myth is the one about women wanting to control men. Historically, women have seen themselves as so powerless that when they try to exert any power at all, it may come out as a roar.

Or, they use a metaphorical cannon when a BB gun would do. I'm not happy about the use of weaponry in this metaphor, however, this is an effort to point out the extreme of what it sometimes takes for a woman to feel she has power. Real power isn't loud. It's not necessary to 'roar' if it's truly felt and owned. The other side of this coin is that men are 'whipped.' Where is the collaboration or allowance that he might just be trying to meet her needs and improve their relationship? Much has been written about the probable historical—and more inclusive—roles of women and men in cave times. It's believed that men could have been involved in rearing children and tending to the cave, and women could have been out there hunting alongside the cavemen. We have assumed roles as if they are set in stone. No pun intended. We are so quick to go to a place of judgment about so many things, including power and control. I often think men have it harder. I never thought the purpose of the Women's Movement was to put men in a subordinate, subservient role to women. If we felt oppressed, would we really want to become the oppressors? I don't believe this is true in most cases. When it's pointed out that it might be occurring, most people are responsive to the possibility and to changing it.

● ● ●

Defining Healthy Relationships

How Do We Choose a Partner?

Instead of focusing on what goes wrong, I'd like to talk about how we might do it right. When we buy a house, we look into it very thoroughly. We usually find a realtor to show us the houses we are interested in, the school district we want to live in, the areas we find desirable and provide the comps to make sure the price is fair. Once we find a house, we negotiate a price we and the seller can agree upon, find out how high the taxes are, search out the best interest rate we can find, hire inspectors to determine if the house is in good repair, find a lender, insure the house, establish a method for paying the mortgage, and so on.

Do we do anything close to this much investigation when we choose a partner? I suggest we don't. Please don't get me wrong; I don't mean to imply that this is a business deal. I do however, submit that a commitment in a relationship deserves at least as much time, effort and learning as does buying a house. Sadly enough, people often neglect to do this. I do understand that the heart wants what the heart wants. I also realize that choosing a partner is a very emotional decision. However, it is important to address practicality, and few people take the time to do this. Perhaps we don't want to be talked out of what the heart wants.

I see this with single people who become sexually involved with someone without finding out if the other person is sexually healthy. Of course that interferes with the flow of going with the moment and the passion. On the other hand, STIs and STDs are very common, and the level of denial which must be present to ignore that is alarming. One of the reasons is that most people have a really difficult time talking about sex. As I like to joke, "You can *do* it, you just can't *talk* about it." This often doesn't change as the relationship progresses and even after marriage. So if we can't comfortably talk about sex, even with those we've known for a long enough time to marry, it stands to reason that a new relationship would provide an even greater challenge to having this conversation. Although I totally understand this, I've seen some very painful and sometimes catastrophic fallout result. I believe that a part of this is our difficulty in taking care of ourselves. We don't want to appear "selfish" or treat sexual intimacy like a business transaction. I do believe there are ways to have this conversation, which speak to concern not only for ourselves, but for our partners as well. An example might be, "We seem to be headed in the direction of greater sexual intimacy, and about that I'm truly happy. For both our sakes, I think it's important that we have a conversation about our sexual health and how recently we have been checked out. Are you comfortable with discussing that with me?"

By the way, whenever I suggest how people might say something, I always encourage them to use their own words instead of mine. Everyone must decide on their own style and comfort level. This is true across the board, not just regarding sex. And while we're on the subject, I want to make clear that when I say "sex" I am talking about sexual intimacy not just intercourse. I have noticed that many people substitute the word "sex" for intercourse. They are not synonymous!

If we branch out beyond sexual intimacy to look at how we learn about our partners, many questions come to mind. Do I know what's important to me? Do I know if my partner shares the same mindset? Do we both agree on whether or not to have children? Do we share similar views on money regarding spending, saving and the freedom of individual choice vs. collaboration? If I am a left-leaning liberal, does it matter if my partner is a staunch Republican? Does religion play a part for either one of us in terms of compatibility and/or childrearing? How different or similar are our backgrounds? If there is a large disparity in our backgrounds, can we be comfortable operating in a world we've never inhabited before or not? Are we sexually compatible? If there's a great difference in our sex drives, have we had conversations about how to work that out in a mutually satisfactory way? Socially, how are we the same, and how do we differ—extrovert vs. introvert? Do we like each other's friends? Family? How compatible are we in terms of our need for space? If we're not compatible, can we comfortably tolerate those differences in one another?

This is not by any means a complete list. Nor is the list in order of importance. It's just a suggestion of some of the issues which might arise to cause difficulties in the relationship. No two people will be completely compatible in all areas. This is where priorities have to be established by each and discussed with the other. So often, we hear what we want to hear and move on from there. This is human nature, and we're not to be faulted for being human. That said, the more we can learn, discuss, negotiate and plan, the better equipped we are for a positive outcome.

How we go about choosing a partner is in great part unconscious. Harville Hendrix, in *Getting the Love You Want: A Guide for Couples*, wrote about what he calls the "Imago." In psychological terms, this is known as the repetition compulsion. We very often seek out what's comfortable and familiar, even if it creates distress and disharmony in the process. For example, if you had a mother who was emotionally smothering and without boundaries, you might very well unconsciously choose a partner with similar traits. Or, if you had a father who was emotionally distant, you might be likely to choose a partner who is also emotionally unavailable. The unconscious goal is to get a better result this time than you were able to achieve with your parent or parents. This seems counterintuitive to most people. Why would I want someone who gives me something I don't want or fails to give me something I do? It all gets back to the original imprinting and the powerlessness we feel as children to change our parents into becoming what we want and need.

The healthier our choice in a partner, and the healthier we are, the more likely we are to get a better outcome. If we choose someone who is too much like our unsatisfactory parent or parents, we will be very unlikely to get better results this time. Of course, that doesn't stop us from trying! Here's my favorite metaphor for this. We're walking down the street, and we see an apple tree. We think, hmm, an apple would taste good right about now. So we walk up to the tree to look for an apple in its branches. Failing to find one, we think, well, maybe an apple fell to the ground, and we look around the tree for an apple. Finally, having no luck in finding an apple, we shake the tree in hopes that perhaps there's an apple in one of the higher branches which we can't see, but can shake loose. Nothing falls. We finally give up and walk on without an apple. At some future time, we find ourselves on that same road again and encounter that same apple tree. Once more, we go through all the steps trying to find the apple, still, with no luck. The same results occur. We repeat this process as many times as necessary until hopefully, we come to the realization that even though it's an apple tree, it has no apples. At that point, we cease to try to find the apple from the source which doesn't provide it.

If you find someone with good boundaries who is loving and nurturing without being smothering and who is independent but available and connected, then you have your relationship apple! You may not find yourself attracted to this initially. The right mix, over time, has the potential to turn into multiple, consecutive apples—maybe even enough for an apple pie!

Keep in mind that the search for the apple begins in childhood with our parents. Long into adulthood we can keep hoping and searching for what we want from them—*willing* them to change. Of course, this never works. The only person we have the power to change is ourselves. Once we can finally accept that in relationships, we change the 'dance.' Then, the other can no longer continue the old dance with us. If a parent is to change, we have to be the ones to initiate the new dance. We have no control over whether or not they choose to come and dance with us.

This is where 'First Me' and 'Then You' play an important role. It is also a place where being responsive vs. responsible comes into focus along with the important distinction between them. We give to ourselves and to our partners because of needs and wants— ours and theirs. If we give too much, go too far and sacrifice our own well-being, we will become impoverished and resentful. It will widen the gap between us. If we don't give sufficiently, it will also widen the gap when our partner does not feel their needs are important. 'Responsible' means I'm in charge of you and your happiness. 'Responsive' means I will care about and address your needs *as long as it is not at my expense.* Most importantly, we don't lose ourselves by taking responsibility for someone else, yet we are responsive to that someone's needs and wants. The line is often difficult to discern. However, the definitive point is when giving to someone else means not taking care of ourselves, and when the expense is so great that it will be damaging for us.

Basic Tenets of Coupledom

There are some 'basic tenets of coupledom' which are important to know and live by. They include (but aren't limited to) the following: Relationships are not tit for tat. If we give with an expectation of receiving in kind, it won't work. Our vulnerabilities and needs are not always the same as our partner's. Competition gets us into trouble—if one wins, both lose. Anger does not mean hatred. Whatever our differences, we're both vulnerable human beings. We are playing for the same 'team.'

In Brene Brown's *The Power of Vulnerability,* which I consider to be one of the most comprehensive and powerful discourses on that subject, she stated that,

> "Connection is what gives purpose and meaning to our lives. It's how we're wired, and why we're here. Shame (the universal fear that there is something about us that if known or seen would deem us unworthy of connection) is what unravels connection. These are the things we don't want to talk about. But, the less we do, the stronger they become."

She further states, "The underpinning of this is excruciating vulnerability. Since we have to let ourselves be really seen in order for connection to happen, the fear and shame can create isolation instead of connection." In her research, she found that people who have a sense of worthiness have a strong sense of love and belonging versus those who struggle with feeling worthy. They always wonder if they're good enough. Her contention is that what separates these two ways of being is the *belief* that they're worthy or the absence of that belief. "Those who believe themselves worthy are courageous enough to be imperfect, have compassion to treat themselves and others kindly and authentically, and are willing to let go of who they thought they should be." I want to emphasize the concept of courageousness, since it's a big part of what this book is all about. When a person can hold to this, despite the discomfort, it becomes not only tolerable, but in fact, may even foster the belief that 'what makes them vulnerable also makes them beautiful.' I find this to be a goal well worth striving for. It's the willingness to take risks with no guarantees of a positive outcome, or in other words to surrender control. Of course this results in vulnerability. Brown says this is the "birthplace of joy, creativity, belonging and love." Unfortunately many people struggle against vulnerability at considerable cost. Defending against it may entail numbing, and as I said earlier, we lose the good feelings as well. According to Brown, when we feel the loss of the good, "we numb again, and this becomes a truly vicious cycle." This is where perfectionism is likely to kick in. Unable to acknowledge our flaws and vulnerability we have little alternative but to strive to be perfect and attempt to create an unreal world in which that model of perfection fits. Brown's 'solution' is "to learn to believe for ourselves and teach our children that we are imperfect, yet worthy of love and belonging. We let ourselves be seen, and love 'wholeheartedly.'" She concludes with the notion that "to feel this vulnerable illuminates our aliveness and helps us believe that we're enough"—or in my favorite terms, 'good enough.' With this courage, we open the door not only to power, but to the necessary ingredients for achieving self-love.

As I often do, I find this concept captured beautifully in music. Specifically, Dan Hill's 1977 hit, *Sometimes When We Touch,* has had millions of views on YouTube, which speaks to the universality of vulnerability. The song speaks of fear, insecurity, and the desire to hide from feelings of tenderness and vulnerability. Rod Stewart recorded it in 2014. The song and message live on. If you haven't heard it, I hope you will.

Another more recent song, *'Like I'm Gonna Lose You'* by Meghan Trainor and featuring John Legend, addresses the vulnerability to loss inherent in love in any and all relationships. Since it is inevitable that loss will eventually occur because mortality is always a factor, the message, much like Tim McGraw's, *Live Like You Were Dying*, is to hold on to those we love and be as conscious as possible of being in the moment, since tomorrow is not a promise but a gift. We really *don't* know when we'll run out of time. Far from being a downer, I find these messages inspirational about how to fully *live.* As far as we know, this is not a 'dress rehearsal,' but the real deal, whatever your beliefs about an afterlife.

Here are some additional tenets from Gottman from the *Psychology Today* article. In looking at what makes relationships succeed, Gottman refers to his random thoughts such as: a good sex life and sense of humor are key; trust is essential; behave like good friends, and handle conflicts in a gentle, positive way; be able to repair negative interactions during an argument; be able to process negative emotions fully. He has also defined the most toxic aspects of a relationship which include criticism, defensiveness, stonewalling, and the most poisonous of all, contempt. The message from the toxic list is to avoid those behaviors/attitudes in order to promote and maintain a good, healthy and happy relationship!

Since Gottman uses mathematical terms often when assessing couples and working with them, a recent statistic, again from the *Psychology Today* article cited above is very relevant. He contends that (generously) assuming that couples are emotionally available to each other fifty percent of the time, the probability that both will be emotionally available at the same time is only twenty-five percent. That's a very small number and means that seventy-five percent (the majority) of the time, couples are operating in a 'minefield' of all sorts of misses which can lead to negative emotions, conflict and outcomes. No wonder it's such a challenge!

Defining Intimacy

The dictionary defines intimacy as "a close, familiar, and usually affectionate or loving personal relationship with another person or group." This definition would include things such as closeness, vulnerability and openness, and is not just reserved for romantic relationships. Although that says it pretty well, there's another popular definition I like even better, "in-to-me-see," which Mizrahi referenced in her article on intimacy. The idea of letting someone see into you and you seeing into them does a better job than the dictionary of making this concept clear. It can also scare the dickens out of people at times!

People often are speaking of sexual intimacy when they refer to intimacy, but those two are not synonymous any more than are sex and intercourse. Michael J. Russer, a prostate cancer survivor, gave an excellent TED Talk on the subject of intimacy entitled *Creating Extraordinary Intimacy in a Shutdown World.* After his prostatectomy, he was unable to achieve an erection. Instead of performance, he learned to focus on being present. He determined that (sexual) intimacy is about "having an open heart, being vulnerable, playful and sexually adventurous." He also discovered that slowing 'way, way down' to please his partner was an exceptionally important and satisfying experience for him, as well as for her. This is a very important message for a man to receive about pleasing a woman, as is his conclusion that "how a man defines himself as a man is a choice." It doesn't have to be about a function, size or many other metrics men are taught to use. He mentioned that when he asked men to define intimacy, they usually responded with, "Sex." As you may have guessed by now, women more often responded with things like "Cuddling, hugging and kissing." Intimacy may include all of these, but it is also an emotional state that does not necessarily include touch at all. Think of close relationships with friends and family not typically physical beyond a hug for 'hello' and 'good-bye.' These relationships may be very close and intimate; however, they are so primarily on the basis of non-physical exchanges.

Since intimacy may or may not include sexual intimacy, one of the things making sexual intimacy in a loving partnership so powerful and wonderful is that, at its best, it is an all-inclusive sense of connection, knowing, and being known physically, emotionally and intellectually. It has the potential to rise to the greatest heights and provide the most profound sense of togetherness possible between two people.

· · ·

Let's Talk about S-E-X

I can't resist beginning this with an anonymous quote: "Sex is dirty, filthy, disgusting and dangerous, which is why you should save it for the one you love." This points not only to the notion that sex is bad before marriage (and all the connotations to go with that), but also the assumption that after marriage (or true love), it will suddenly be not only good but great—and it will be easy to flip that switch. If you're told that sex is bad before marriage, it's pretty hard to remove the 'sex is bad' part once you *are* married. While the expectations have changed for many, there are still those who adhere to this belief, and as a result, it's rarely smooth sailing.

As a sex therapist, I would be greatly remiss if I did not include sexual development and sexuality as a part of this book. Sexuality is something we are born with and do not need to be taught. Unfortunately, due to cultural and often parental discomfort with the notion of children as sexual beings, the messages given to children about their sexuality may be very negative and introduce the notion that sexuality is bad, which is not easily discarded.

Religion often has a big impact upon children and adults, as well. Brittany and Christopher were high school sweethearts who attended the same college (which was affiliated with their religion.) Although they managed to enjoy each other in a sexual relationship, it was quite circumscribed and did not include intercourse or oral sex. When they married, neither had experience other than what they had learned together. Both were disappointed by their first sexual intimacy experiences as a married couple. Since both shared the same religious upbringing, they became disenchanted with the teachings their parents held so dear. The result was fallout in their relationships with their parents. They had followed the rules almost to the letter, but the magic didn't happen.

Their anger and disappointment led them away from religion and into continued disharmony with their parents. They entered therapy in hopes of achieving a mutually satisfying sexual relationship. Brittany was very inhibited and self-conscious about her body, which increased her difficulty in being engaged during sexual intimacy. Prior to their marriage, she had found it much easier to be relaxed and enjoy herself sexually, but having all her clothes off left her feeling very vulnerable and self-conscious. Christopher had no idea how to help her with this. He experienced erectile dysfunction at times, and eager ejaculation any time they had intercourse. They were both lost and feeling hopeless and helpless. With time, education, conversation and resources, both began to learn about their own sexuality, as well as their spouse's. It took quite a while for them to begin to redefine themselves as sexual beings and to be able to see that as a positive thing. In times of stress, the old messages would come to the fore. They felt hopeless again, at times. But eventually, they reached a point of comfort with their bodies and their sexuality, and they were able to leave therapy with information and a comfortable sense of rightness instead of shame in matters sexual. In addition, to the extent possible, they were able to repair their family of origin relationships, however neither had regained a religious affiliation at the time they completed therapy.

It certainly appears that sex is 'coming out of the closet,' and I am happy to see that! The Supreme Court ruling on same sex marriages, Caitlin Jenner's interview regarding her lack of gender conformity and all the attendant pain, the book, *Fifty Shades of Grey*, and *Sticky: A (Self) Love Story* (about masturbation) are some significant examples. For those who may not be familiar with the book, (*Fifty Shades* is actually a trilogy,) it is a romance novel, which contained BDSM (sexual dominance and submission) practices. The folks who do not practice this (which constitute the majority) are considered 'plain-vanilla.' Vanilla sex, or some variation of that, is what most couples engage in. Once again, I want to be clear when speaking of any population that there is no judgment about any practices anyone chooses to participate in, either in or out of the category of vanilla. I bring this up both to heighten awareness, as well as to mention what I consider to be one very important related subject. Those who are involved in BDSM have very clear rules and forms of communication, as well as contracts that both participants consent to. *Consent* is the operative word. Unlike many in the 'vanilla' world, they *do* talk about sex—in great detail, in fact. It would be terrific if the vanilla people could take a page out of that book. In other words, if two people could sit down while not engaged in the throes of lovemaking, and talk about what they like, what they don't like, how they would like to communicate with or be communicated with during sexual intimacy and how they might refuse in such a manner so as to be clear but not create a feeling of rejection in their partner. The real truth is that saying no means taking care of oneself and is not meant to hurt or reject the other.

These are some suggested topics for conversation. However many other things might be included such as sexual fantasies, possible interest in role-playing or anything else that might be important for either party. So often when one person wants to be sexually intimate and is turned down by their partner they walk away feeling rejected and unwanted. Part of this is the manner in which they are told, as well as the absence of communication between them about what might feel better to hear. Back to my earlier comment about couples being able to do it but not talk about it;

being able to talk would make a world of difference. Often, the person saying "no" feels guilty, so they may sound harsher than they intend. If the guilt is there, anger may be, as well. In other words, "I wish you hadn't asked so I didn't have to turn you down and feel badly about it!" Nonverbal communication is also an important part of lovemaking, as are affection and perhaps most importantly, connection. Nonverbal cues can be used in negative ways, which constitute a boundary violation. We are sensitive to the look on our partner's face, raised eyebrows, rolling eyes, pursed lips and a multitude of other nonverbal messages. Although I said earlier that communication is most effective in person, negative communication, including nonverbal cues can carry a mighty punch.

Sometimes opening up possibilities can also open communication. The more you can talk about sex, the better the experience is likely to become. It's perfectly okay to talk about it in the bedroom, however, it's often easier to talk about it elsewhere. Women seem to have more difficulty talking about it, generally speaking, but that doesn't mean guys are necessarily at ease in that area either.

Women's Sexuality

Recently I came up with the concept of 'Women's Sexuality Emancipation Proclamation.' What does this mean? I believe that women frequently hand over their sexuality to the male in their lives. At first glance, this might sound strange, but think about it. This often begins much earlier than in adult relationships, oftentimes in adolescence. Back to toxic gender mythology—"She's a tease" is a judgment females fear, along with being seen as withholding, or using sex for power or control. Therefore, as stated earlier, she will usually feel she must at least maintain sexual practices with her partner, once they are established.

Okay, now I'll talk about bases, but I've never really understood the universal (if it exists) definition of what constitutes first, second, or third base. I'm pretty sure intercourse would be a home run, but even that is open to question! So to spell it out, if he gets to second base once, he always gets to second base in the future, and so on. This is the place where a sense of being in charge of her sexuality is at risk of beginning to erode for the woman. There's an unwritten, unspoken law between two heterosexual people to that effect. Marriage or a committed relationship heightens it all. Then it's a 'wifely duty,' she 'wouldn't want him to find it somewhere else,' etc.

It's not surprising that before long sex may become obligatory. Ownership of her sexuality is often forfeited and is given to him. She wants him to be pleased and feels guilty and worried if he's not. I so often hear women say they submit, put up with, and resent doing it, and I often hear that they would be perfectly happy to never have sex again. Wow. That's such a powerful statement. To me, it usually means she's either lost touch with or never got in touch with her own sexuality. Women talk of depriving men, but rarely speak of depriving themselves. It's as though they cease to see themselves as sexual beings.

Once on this path of erosion, her sexuality increasingly belongs less and less to herself. Self-pleasuring may also cease. Women often feel that if they're not being sexual with their partner, it's certainly not okay for them to be sexual with themselves. Or, if they are, they tend to feel guilty about it. So they may just shut it down altogether, and it's as if they never had it to begin with. If you think about it, you'll realize this is a tremendous loss for anyone. It may not be conscious, but if a woman has relinquished her own sexuality, sexual intimacy no longer serves to meet *her* needs, only his. That disassociation with one's own sexuality almost inevitably ends in experiencing oneself as asexual. Although asexuality does exist, that isn't the case here. It's simply an end point to a destructive process.

The way I conceptualize this sexual shutdown, which I frequently see in my practice, is as the loss of sexual identity. In our culture, as well as many others, women are socialized in such a way as to give away their sexuality to the male in their lives. I want to be very clear that this is not a blame statement for men, nor for women.

Lauren is an unfortunate example of someone who exemplifies both giving up her own sexuality and putting another's needs ahead of her own at her expense. She barely tolerates intercourse with her husband. Sometimes she bleeds afterwards, since she is not sexually aroused or lubricated. She feels obligated, as his wife, to give her husband what he desires sexually, no matter how she feels. She does not speak up about her pain or about what she needs to be aroused and receptive to penetration. Lauren is in her twenties, part of an age demographic whose increasing use of lubricants has been noted with surprise. The theory postulated is that more young people today forego foreplay and go straight to intercourse than in generations before. My speculation is that the art of making out may be getting lost. Along with that goes the progression of intimacy generally needed for female sexual arousal. So Lauren is far from alone, both in terms of suffering in silence and in not knowing how to remedy the situation.

Ironically, women are missing out not only on what they are not getting, but completely unaware of what that represents for them. This, of course, is not the case for all women, but is quite often true for women who are not interested in being sexual with their partners. I encourage women to discover or re-discover their own sexuality and to leave him out of the equation until it's found, and it once again belongs to them! Ultimately, this benefits not only the woman, but her partner who almost never wants obligatory sex.

As stated, this loss of sexual identity does not happen to every female, but it happens too frequently to be ignored. Understanding it, whatever your gender, can be a huge help in changing and moving past it.

Other things capable of interfering with a woman's sexuality include some seldom talked about painful conditions they may experience, which are much more common than people realize (because they're not often talked about). Some examples are vaginismus, vulvodynia and pelvic floor pain. Vaginismus is an involuntary contraction of vaginal muscles making penetration impossible. If penetration of any kind is attempted, it is experienced as very painful. This wreaks havoc with a woman's self-esteem and sexuality. If she has a partner who also doesn't understand it, both are at a loss for a solution. Treatment for this condition is not only available, but most often successful.

Experiencing pain is sometimes not disclosed by a woman to her partner. There are any number of reasons why she may be reluctant to tell him. In situations like this, once he finds out, he almost always feels guilty about inflicting pain and sometimes resentful of not being told. It's so important for a woman to disclose this, and to be aware that it's ultimately better for both not to keep silent and that help can be obtained.

Traditionally, women have had a difficult time asking for what they want and need in general. This certainly applies in the sexual arena, if asking or if saying no is already a challenge. Sadly, I still see this with young women who are able to be assertive in their careers and other aspects of their lives, but not when it comes to their partner, and especially not when it comes to sex.

I want to mention here that it is not infrequent for the man to be the one less interested in sexual intimacy. I will say more about this later, but I don't want to continue without stating that explicitly, especially since it is much less talked about. Therefore, it's even more important that it be 'on the record.'

When either partner does not want to be sexual with the other, it constitutes a great paradox for sex therapy. In fact, I often ask both partners to 'take sex off the table' in the beginning. This almost always seems counterintuitive, which is quite understandable. Why would a sex therapist encourage you *not* to have sex? By the time a couple reaches my therapy room, sex has become at best a source of pain and at worst, a matter of contention, sometimes with divorce or ending the relationship being considered by one or both. Continuing a non-productive pattern serves no useful purpose, so the goal is to interrupt the 'dance' and create a new one.

One suggestion I do make is that touch and affection take place even if the couple is not engaging sexually. Affection goes out the door the moment someone is seeking to avoid sexual intimacy for fear that it 'will lead to something else.' So, in addition to the loss of a sexual connection, the couple becomes distant physically. This only serves to widen the gulf between them.

Returning to the model of the woman having low or no libido and the man being much more interested in sexual intimacy, it's often the case that the woman has been accommodating his needs for a long time—sometimes many decades. I encourage women to find and keep their sexuality for themselves, with the eventual goal of including their partner in a sexually intimate manner. In the meantime, I encourage men to 'cease and desist' any and all actions, comments, jokes, etc. with a sexual component in order to make it 'safe' for their partner to be both physically and emotionally close to him without fear that it 'will lead to something else.' Unless the male partner has a problem with masturbation, (which does happen, although rarely) I encourage him to be responsible for his own sexual pleasure during this time of abstinence between them. Although you might assume the man would have the greater objection to this new, yet temporary, dance, it is often the woman who will protest. Won't that just make things worse and upset him all the more? When a man understands that this is what his partner needs in order for there to be the possibility (and it's *not* a certainty) that they can achieve a mutually consensual, pleasurable and satisfying level of sexual intimacy, most are willing, and sometimes even eager to participate. It's important that neither approaches this as possessing a guaranteed outcome, or the pressure of that may interfere with the possibility that it will occur.

Robert and Lisa were married for thirty years when they first came to see me. Lisa was a virgin when they married, and Robert had some experience sexually, but not a great deal. Lisa had never had an orgasm and never could understand why sexual intimacy was such a big deal to Robert and, seemingly, the rest of the world. She stated, "I would be perfectly happy in my marriage, if it wasn't for his wanting to have sex." Although she did feel sexual arousal at times when they were making love, she never 'got' what a peak experience might be. She was fine with stopping as soon as Robert was finished, which she encouraged to be as short a time as possible. Robert felt inadequate when trying to give her sexual pleasure. His feelings of inadequacy were sprinkled with resentment that she wouldn't (but in fact couldn't) tell him what she wanted. Somehow, he thought it was incumbent upon him to figure it out. He thought he had failed her as a lover, and he also thought nothing would ever change. After all, thirty years is a long time.

With the help of therapy, books, videos and 'toys,' Lisa was able to achieve an orgasm on her own. It took some time before she was ready to include Robert in her newfound sexual domain. Once she was comfortable enough to do so, the results were very satisfying for both. Together they learned more about sexual expression and variation, and most importantly, what each of them wanted and found enjoyable, as well as what worked for their partner. They also found their increased sexual intimacy greatly enhanced their emotional intimacy, and both reported experiencing a level of connection they had never before experienced. Hence, a very 'happy ending!'

A common problem for both men and women is the inability to stay in their bodies and in the physicality of the sexual experience. They 'go up in their heads,' as I call it. Once they're in their heads, they've left their bodies. It becomes difficult, if not impossible to enjoy the experience, let alone have an orgasm. This, of course, does not include sexual fantasies that may increase arousal, but a moving away from sexual thoughts to performance, unrelated topics, etc. will almost always get in the way. One metaphor I use for this is to imagine a bubble (as in the kind you blow as a child) in which the interrupting thoughts are contained and letting the bubble carry the thoughts away, allowing them to re-focus on their bodies and sensations.

A highly useful 'tool' for helping couples like Lisa and Robert, as well as anyone who has difficulty staying in their physical experience is sensate focus, developed by William Masters, M.D.

and Virginia Johnson. Masters and Johnson first published the seminal work, *Human Sexual Response* in 1966, which was later updated, and their contributions represented a huge breakthrough in providing scientific information about sexuality. Although there are different versions and interpretations of sensate focus, I find the most effective one is non-sexual touch with a focus on temperature, texture and pressure. Erogenous zones are totally off limits, so the areas of touch exclude them, and each partner has a turn (usually for a mutually predetermined period of time, e.g. five minutes, ten minutes), and both the person doing the touching and the one receiving the touch maintain a focus only on those three things: temperature, texture and pressure. This is truly a way to be in touch with your body, your sensations and to learn to block out distracting thoughts. Ideally, it does not lead to sexual intimacy although there is no ban on becoming sexually aroused should that occur. If both want to be sexual with each other after a sensate focus exercise, they take a break first and then engage sexually. Therefore, there is no future expectation that the two experiences will be linked. As one person so appropriately put it, "Come back to your senses!"

Goal oriented lovemaking gets in the way of sexual, sensual and emotional fulfillment. Having an orgasm is not a prerequisite to enjoying a sexual encounter. Many men (and some women) have a difficult time understanding or believing this. In most cases, no one objects to an orgasm. Nonetheless, an experience of sexual intimacy without orgasm or intercourse can be very enjoyable and fulfilling. Oftentimes a woman feels pressure to have an orgasm, sometimes because she fears he will feel he's not a good lover if she doesn't. This is ironic, and once again, it's the woman putting the man's needs ahead of her own, which might be just to relax and enjoy whatever happens. Well-intentioned though his desire for her to orgasm may be, if she feels pressure, it backfires. It is *her* orgasm! If they both stay focused on the experience instead of the outcome, things are much more likely to be satisfying to both.

As men age, they sometimes have difficulty having an orgasm, or they may have difficulty with orgasms for reasons other than aging. The more this is focused upon, the more it becomes a problem. 'Performance anxiety' is the term frequently used to describe erectile dysfunction or eager ejaculation for a man, but can include any aspect of being sexual, including delayed ejaculation. What's seldom talked about is a woman's performance anxiety. Of course it manifests somewhat differently, since arousal is not essential (although highly desirable) for a woman to engage in intercourse. However, the most common form of performance anxiety is a woman's fear that she won't be adequately aroused in order to enjoy the sexual experience. Or, she may worry about losing focus and veering away from her arousal due to any number of things. Instead of losing touch with her body, she may become self-conscious and focused on her body image in a negative manner that interferes with staying in the moment, and still winds up taking herself out of the physical experience and enjoyment. An interesting side note here is from an article I read some time ago in which studies indicated that women were quite likely to focus on their own bodies during lovemaking (not in a positive way), whereas men were not tuned into that same station but were instead more absorbed by the experience with their partner. Good to know for women! It's important that women and men understand how anxiety regarding lovemaking can interfere with their pleasure. Most women know they must treat their male partner gently when he experiences any sexual difficulty, but not everyone (including women) is aware of that same need for a woman. I suggest that if either is feeling anxious, it's a good time to acknowledge that, or if that's too difficult, to ask to pause in the lovemaking and just hold each other until it (hopefully) passes. I hope you will 'relax and enjoy.' That's a good enough 'goal' for anyone!

Some women have never experienced an orgasm. They often see themselves as defective in some way, which enhances all things negative about their own sexuality and their sexual relationships. This, along with the internal and external 'pressure,' often results in them faking orgasms. This is a no-win situation, not only creating deception and guilt, but often the suspicion or at least uncertainty on the man's part as to what's really happening. If her partner suspects she's faking, he may feel he's not a 'good enough' lover, so both miss out on an authentic sexual relationship and the opportunity to explore together how an orgasm for her becomes possible. There are a number of books on this subject, but I especially recommend *For Yourself: The Fulfillment of Female Sexuality* by Lonnie Barbach because it focuses on the idea of sexuality belonging to a woman. She does an excellent job of helping women learn to become orgasmic. In fact, she states that every woman with a clitoris (with rare exceptions) is capable of having an orgasm. Another excellent book on the subject of orgasms is *Becoming Orgasmic: A Sexual and Personal Growth Program for Women* by Julia Heiman and Joseph LoPiccolo.

As women age, hormonal and physiological changes occur which can impact sexual functioning. This does not mean sexuality or orgasm comes to an end! I'm amazed by how many people seem to believe that is so. In fact, there is no reason why people can't continue to enjoy some version of sexuality for their entire lives—and yes, I do realize many are living to be one hundred years old or more. Our biggest driver of libido is our brain. Our biggest sex 'organ' is our skin. Even with Alzheimer's, when the brain shrinks and mental function declines, I actually witnessed a woman sitting on the lap of a man in a wheelchair on an Alzheimer's unit and planting a big kiss on his mouth until the attendants told her to stop. Perhaps sex-ed for caregivers to the elderly might come in handy in this regard!

An important note here: when someone comes to me with a sexual issue which might be physiological in nature, the first step is to find out if it is. I don't presume that all problems are psychological in origin, although certainly a physical problem is very likely to cause an emotional reaction.

A bit more about male sexual function needs to be said. Men who have difficulty attaining or maintaining erections have certainly had the opportunity to feel they're not alone with the many television commercials on this topic. What some men don't know; however, is that you don't have to be 'older' to experience this phenomenon. I encourage anyone who is concerned about this to consult a physician, as well as the abundant literature available. The same applies to what is now known as 'eager ejaculation.' These are issues that cause great concern and sometimes shame for those who experience them. Be heartened by the fact that they are remediable. Two books I find particularly comprehensive and helpful are *The New Male Sexuality*, by Bernie Zilbergeld, and *Male Sexuality: Why Women Don't Understand It—And Men Don't Either*, by Michael Bader.

Earlier I spoke of what transpires prior to sexual intimacy as either leading toward or away from it. To me, this makes perfect sense. If you're angry or distant from each other, it is often difficult to find your way back to the intimacy. The exception, of course, would be 'make-up sex.' I suspect that works best when some tender words are spoken first, but sometimes it happens in the reverse order. Then there are those who don't even relate to the idea of make-up sex at all. Sex is not a conduit to making up for them; it is something which might occur after they patch things up.

One of the things I often share with men is that for most women, the first part of actual foreplay often begins in meaningful conversation. When the conversation leads to a feeling of closeness and connection, women are generally more receptive to sexual intimacy because emotional intimacy has been established. John Gray, author of *Men are from Mars, Women are from Venus*, says that men open up emotionally with sex. I've checked that one out with many men I've seen professionally, and I haven't found one yet who disagreed with that premise. So if it's true that women open up to sex by feeling close first and men open up and feel close during and after sex, it begins to be very clear that each gender is coming from a different direction. Although a challenge, this is not insurmountable as long as the couple understands what differences might exist and endeavors to give their partner what they need. Maybe this is why some men tell me they're simple; most men (although not all, and oftentimes this changes as men get older) are fine with a woman touching their penis before anything else happens between them. On the other hand, most women do not want to be touched in their erogenous zones (breasts, genitals) until they have had time to warm up to the idea. Or, to quote Dr. Gray again, "Women are like ovens; they have to be pre-heated for fifteen minutes. Men are like blowtorches."

In more instances than not, I agree with William Masters: When things don't work well in the bedroom, they don't work well in the living room either.

Libido (Sexual Drive)

The sexual drive and frequency of desire differs among individuals. This may ebb and flow within a person during the course of their lifetime, but there is no 'normal' (something I refer to as a setting on a washing machine). When a couple is out of sync in this area, it often creates problems and disharmony. It's rare that a couple is matched in this regard, and as stated, this match may change over time. At the beginning of a sexual relationship, the drive and frequency of desire is likely to be strong and often. This usually subsides to some extent over time as the relationship continues. Ideally, the excitement of the newness becomes replaced by the deepening of the intimacy shared by the couple. Over time, they have shared experiences, history, family ties, etc., all of which potentially lead to not only a greater sense of knowing each other, but to a heightened state of excitement and fulfillment, i.e. a much more evolved sense of physical and emotional intimacy. I am often met with skepticism when I make that statement, but there are people who not only will have that experience, but will confirm that this is so.

I remember watching a couple being interviewed about their sexual relationship during my training in marriage and family therapy. The therapist asked each of them the following question, "How many times a day do you want to have sexual intimacy?" He asked the man first, who replied, "Two to four times." He then turned to the woman, asked the same question, and her response was, "One to two times." The therapist deliberately made an assumption that each would like to have sexual intimacy every day. It was interesting that both responded in the affirmative, even if not in the same number of times. I have occasionally asked this of couples, and I'm always interested in the responses I get. The presumption that everyone would want to be sexual every day is obviously not correct. That it would be perfectly okay if they did is embedded in the way the question was phrased.

What happens when a couple is significantly out of sync with each other in this regard? Very often guilt, blame, rejection, and resentment occur. I view this as taking a fundamental individual function personally. The quest for whose frequency of sexual desire is 'normal' is something I often see with couples. The need to see themselves as okay will cause them to label their partner in some negative way. "She is a nymphomaniac. There's something wrong with him! She's frigid. All he cares about is sex," are just a few of the many accusations I've heard leveled against people's partners in the name of truth and in the pursuit of being the 'right' one. This is not only competitive; it is destructive to the relationship. Sadly, we aren't taught any of this. So our expectation that we will both want the same thing at the same time is unmet. Because this is so often the case in the beginning stages of relationships, that expectation is reinforced. When this ebbs over time, we seek to find an explanation as to why. Simply put, the explanation is that we are all different. Different does not mean right or wrong.

I've stated it's not okay for women to have obligatory sex in order to keep peace. I should add that it's not okay for men either. That doesn't mean that either partner can't choose to give their partner pleasure, even if they themselves are not desirous of being sexual. I understand this may sound like a contradiction, so I'll explain further. There are so many different ways we can give and receive sexual pleasure, and not all roads lead to intercourse. I think it's fine (and even desirable) if someone doesn't really wish to participate, but is on board with the idea of giving their partner pleasure that they do just that. Interestingly, this sometimes becomes arousing for the partner who was not originally interested in being sexual; however, this does not always happen. Research indicates that couples who are able to do this often have a more active and mutually satisfying sexual relationship, as well as a better relationship overall. It makes sense, from the standpoint of potential arousal and engaging sexually in a manner agreeable to both. An article in *Psychology Today* by Jennifer Bleyer, *Good in Bed* refers to this as "...motivation to meet each other's sexual needs, a quality known as sexual communal strength." Some individuals are not comfortable with this alternative, which makes things more challenging. Nevertheless, there is usually some middle ground that can be reached, if only they will talk about it. Suffering in silence is *never* okay.

To clarify the different meanings of desire and arousal regarding sex, desire is the want, and arousal is feeling 'turned on.' It has been postulated that women are much less likely than men to feel desire first before arousal. Desire does occur for women; however, I think it more frequently follows arousal for women than for men. That doesn't mean that same sequencing never happens with men, as it certainly does. It's just more likely to happen more often for women.

As I mentioned earlier, people are often surprised that women don't have a corner on the market of low or no sexual desire. It's important for everyone to know this, since it's much less widely talked about in our culture when the man has lower sexual desire. As a result, even more self-doubt for both people and feelings of rejection for the woman are likely to occur. Men talk to each other about their wives' lack of interest in being sexual as often as they might like. To borrow a quote from actor Kevin Nealon's character in the TV series *Weeds*, "Men whose wives *want* to have sex with them tend not to talk about it." Women, on the other hand, often talk to each other about their husbands' desires to have sexual intimacy more often than them. Therefore, when a man has less interest than his female partner, he tends to think he's the only one (not true) and that perhaps there is something wrong with him. His female partner often feels the same way about herself.

Although the terms low libido and no libido are commonly used in the mental health field, (and although I don't deny that there are people who have little or no interest in being sexual and consider themselves asexual) most of the people I see who have no physical causation are deterred either by relationship issues or difficulties in how they experience their sexuality and/or their bodies. For them, change is quite possible. If a woman has given her sexuality away, her first step is to reclaim it, or in some cases, to claim it for the first time. I don't mean to oversimplify what is a complex issue; however, I do want to be clear that sometimes the solution can be found fairly readily. If the root cause lies within the context of the relationship or some preconceived notion of what and how one 'should' be, learning the causes and finding ways to ameliorate them can be a pathway back to a more mutually satisfying sexual relationship.

Sometimes people will ask me what I suggest to help them trigger sexual arousal and desire. There are some excellent websites, which are erotic but not pornographic. I recommend www.sexsmartfilms.com as well as www.comstockfilms.com. Suggested films from Comstock are Bill and Desiree, and an older couple, Matt & Khym. These films show real people making love and actually talking about their sexual relationship in specific terms. Some films are available to view at no cost, others not.

I very much like the term 'mismatched libidos.' Truth to tell, it would be extremely rare, if not impossible, to find two people with perfectly matched libidos. If that were possible, it would definitely be impossible for them to match every single time, despite the fact that it feels that way for most couples at the beginning of their relationship. However, they don't live together, have spans of time between 'dates,' and if they are sexually intimate, both are generally mutually interested in participating fully in that endeavor most of the times when they're able to be together.

And thus our expectations are set for all that is to come in the future. Since that early passion will inevitably change in most relationships over time, it's vitally important to understand what that's about—and what it's not. As I said previously, I see many couples for whom 'mismatched' libidos are the reason they come to counseling. In the light of gender mythology, disproving of the myths, same gender couples don't identically match either!

Although difficult, being able to recognize that your partner is simply taking care of themselves by having a choice about being sexual or not, can eliminate feelings of rejection. Oftentimes, when this doesn't occur and the couple does not engage in open and clear dialogue to find resolution, the pattern of rejection, guilt, anger and resentment continues indefinitely, sometimes over the entire span of the relationship.

Neil Cannon, Ph.D. and Lisa Thomas, LMFT, both AASECT certified sex therapists, developed a wonderful model for sexual intimacy which I often use with my clients. In a webinar, Dr. Cannon described this concept of a four tier wedding cake. Going from the bottom layer up, it looks like this: connection; kissing and making out; foreplay and intercourse. According to Dr. Cannon, many couples that are struggling sexually have their cake upside down. In other words, they start with intercourse as the foundation instead of the top, last layer. He suggests that couples determine what their wedding cake looks like (even if they're not married!)

and begin a conversation with their partner about whether they both like the way it looks currently or how they want to change it, if necessary.

Sexual Self-Pleasuring

If this were TV, I'd be putting a "Warning: Adult Content—Viewer Discretion Advised" right about here. Hold on to your seats, as I plan to start with how sexuality begins, which, continuing the theme of First Me, is with self-pleasuring, in other words, masturbation.

According to WebMD, *"Masturbation is the first sexual act experienced by most males and females."* In young children, masturbation is a *normal* part of the growing child's exploration of his or her body. Most people continue to masturbate in adulthood, and many do so throughout their lives." Even the word 'masturbation' is fraught with social constraint, embarrassment and inhibition. When a parent observes their child discovering and touching their genitals, a normal part of the growing child's exploration of his or her body, the most common response is some sort of admonition against doing so. It is a knee-jerk reaction not meant to cause harm.

Nonetheless, the child comes away with a sense of shame and wrongdoing in most instances. If a parent were able to plan ahead for this inevitable event, she or he might think in terms of responding differently. One example of how this might go is "It feels very good to touch yourself there. Everyone enjoys that good feeling. It's another one of those things that we do privately, and you can touch yourself as much as you want when you are in your room or being private." Depending on the child's age and the parent's communication style, different words may be used. The important thing is to impart a message to your child that there is nothing wrong, bad or shameful in their behavior. This can often be a stretch for parents; however, if they are prepared beforehand, it makes it easier. Should you be reading this after the fact, it's not too late to go back and revisit the topic with your child. I recently learned that some pediatricians are now instructing parents or giving them pamphlets about how to do this very thing! If you are feeling that shame or are having your own memories of how this was handled in your childhood, please know you have lots of company. Conversely, if you are not aware of ever having sexually self-pleasured, you still have plenty of company.

On the subject of how to handle sexuality in general with children, Esther Perel's blog on this topic had a great deal of wisdom to offer. She stated: "Children who see their primary caregivers at ease expressing affection (within appropriate boundaries) are more likely to embrace sexuality with the healthy combination of respect, responsibility, and curiosity it deserves." She talks about parents' concerns that they protect their children by not exposing them to more than they're ready for. However, she states if the parents' sexuality is censored to an extreme, children inherit the same inhibitions which bind their parents. Finding that middle ground, trusting your instincts, talking with friends and possibly your child's pediatrician are likely to be helpful in figuring it out.

Perel goes on to say that it's important to be truthful and straightforward in order for children to see that sex is not dirty or shameful. She encourages using the terms penis or vagina, as opposed to finding other words. Kids will learn (or incorrectly learn) about sex from peers or online, so give them 'the real story.' She suggests keeping answers short, simple and age appropriate and letting the 'teachable moments' be an entry point to talk about love, sexuality, bodies, etc.

These are some ways for parents to build a common comfort level for both themselves and their children, while laying the groundwork to discuss not only the more challenging topics, but all the things we want our children to learn which they aren't being taught in the classroom. We can usually figure that out by using our own learning deficits as an example!

Until Masters and Johnson's scientific experiments in the late 1950s proved that women were capable of orgasms, there was great uncertainty about whether this was actually possible. It's amazing to see how far we've come from that place of ignorance. Yet, despite over sixty years of research about female sexuality, women are often still in the dark about masturbation. Some women tell me that they have never masturbated. They may not have done so, have forgotten early exploration or feel too ashamed to acknowledge it. Many women have never looked at their own genitals—ever. These females have not learned how to understand, accept and embrace their own bodies and their own sexual make-up. To quote William Masters, "Sex is a natural function. You can't make it happen, but you can teach people to let it happen."

WebM.D. continues,

> "Who Masturbates? Just about everybody. Masturbation is a very common behavior, even among people who have a sex partner. In one national study, 95% of males and 89% of females reported that they have masturbated. . . and most continue . . . into adulthood . . . and many . . . throughout their lives. Why do people masturbate? In addition to feeling good, masturbation is a good way of relieving the sexual tension that can build up over time, especially for people without

partners or whose partners are not willing or available for sex. It also is necessary when a man must give a semen sample for infertility testing or for sperm donation. When sexual dysfunction is present in an adult, masturbation may be prescribed by a sex therapist to allow a person to experience an orgasm (often in women) or to delay its arrival (often in men)."

In 2015 at the annual AASECT (the American Association of Sex Educators, Counselors and Therapists) conference, there was a showing of a then not-yet-released motion picture entitled *Sticky*, about masturbation. The director and creator of the film, Nicholas Tana, had just returned from the Cannes Film Festival, where the film was very well received. The movie is to be released May, 2016. Hopefully this film will allay some of the negative feelings associated with sexual self-pleasuring and bring to light the 'normalcy' of giving this pleasure to oneself.

According to a rabbi in the film, the original source for the proscription against masturbation is to be found in Genesis 38:8-10. The story of Onan is the reason cited. According to the story, Onan's brother passed away, leaving a widow. It was Onan's responsibility to impregnate her, as instructed by God; however, his sister-in-law's children (should he succeed in helping conceive them), would not be 'his' children, so Onan practiced coitus interruptus, withdrawing before orgasm and "spilling his seed on the ground" to prevent a pregnancy. This disobedience and failure to follow God's rule by spilling his seed on the ground was punished by death and became equated with masturbation. To my knowledge, there is no other biblical source prohibiting masturbation.

Interestingly, but not surprisingly, until recent decades it was not even discussed (with the exception of Masters and Johnson) that women might also engage in masturbatory behavior. This is another example of sexism that caused women to feel at least as bad, (if not worse,) about themselves as did men about sexually pleasuring themselves. In addition, since it wasn't even mentioned, a woman would be likely to think she was the only one, and in most cases be too ashamed to talk to anyone about it.

Sex and Porn 'Addiction'

Another very important topic I want to address is the subject of Internet porn. I have seen many couples who come to see me because he 'has a porn addiction.' In Paul and Theresa's case, he had gone to a group for men with sexual addictions. He was not the first I heard say that he felt he didn't belong there along with some who had been referred by the legal system. Theresa felt badly for Paul, since she understood it was a demoralizing experience for him. But like other women I've seen, she didn't know what else to do. So they came to see me. In my profession, there is a great debate as to whether or not sexual addiction is a real thing or not. Many say it does not fit the criteria for an 'addiction,' but instead, at times, may be a compulsion. I'm of that belief. Still others in my field label it 'addiction,' and treat it as such.

There were several important questions I asked Paul in order to determine whether his behavior was compulsive and what might be driving him to the Internet. I wanted to know if he preferred masturbation to being sexually intimate with his wife (which still might not constitute a compulsion but more an expediency or relationship issue or both.) He said he much preferred being sexual with her, but that option had not often been available to him. I asked if he was looking for visual stimulation for the purpose of masturbation, and indeed, he was. In this case, it was more about Theresa's discomfort with the source of visual stimulation and a sense of not being able to live up to the 'perfect' bodies of the women online. Interestingly, many men who view Internet pornography feel the same sense of inadequacy when they compare themselves to the men in these films. As I told Theresa and Paul, those are common feelings. However, they bear little resemblance to the truth. Most makers of pornography are only casting people who are as physically well-endowed as the ones seen on the screen. That does not make them typical! I told Paul and Theresa that the first common source of visual stimulation for people who sought that was *Playboy Magazine*. I doubt anyone ever thought of that as an addiction. My comparison seems to be borne out by the fact that *Playboy* has (at least for now) stopped displaying nudity. Perhaps that's because the time and need for such a vehicle has moved to the Internet.

There are websites that cater to sexual interests falling more into the realm of 'kink,' which are sexually arousing to people with specific preferences. That doesn't necessarily mean they're interested in a real life experience such as that, although sometimes that is the case. Theresa came away with the idea that Paul's interest in Internet pornography did not make him aberrant, nor did it pose a threat to his desire for her. Paul breathed a huge sigh of relief!

In Nancy Friday's books, she offered information about women's sexual fantasies from a large sampling of women, and the first book, *My Secret Garden*, was so successful that she published two more. Women's fantasies ran the gamut of the stuff found in a romance novel to rape and all sorts of other interesting and, at times, surprising ideas. I especially want to mention that those fantasies were sometimes acted out, but just as often not acted upon. I use the rape fantasy as the easiest to understand. Most women would never be desirous of being raped in real life, but in the confines of their own minds (and scripts) it might be both a safe and sexually arousing experience, because they maintain control. Fantasies are much like feelings—judgment-proof. Because all those women found those fantasies sexually arousing, might they be labeled as sex or porn addicts? Possibly the biggest distinction may be that men are less threatened by women's sexual fantasies than many women are by men's or perhaps not that many women share them with their partners!

As for sex addiction, the same question applies as to whether or not it's an actual addiction. However, there are cases of hyper-sexuality which are troublesome to either the individual experiencing it, their partner, or both. This can be addressed in a therapeutic setting to determine its existence and best treatment approaches. Oftentimes, a partner will label their significant other as a 'sex addict' when what is really happening is a discrepancy between frequency of desire on the part of each.

Sexual Orientation and Gender Identity

Why would a man 'choose' to be gay? Why would a five year old 'boy' throw temper tantrums and disobey rules unless 'he' is allowed to wear a dress and become the sweet and agreeable child 'she' is? Why did the Supreme Court rule in favor of same-sex marriage? What's this world coming to?

I have an answer for that last question: The world is coming to its senses. Not easily, not finally and not everyone in it. Since the subjects of sexual orientation and gender identity are often highly emotional, it's not at all surprising that we (in our culture) have a very difficult time understanding and accepting anything out of 'the norm.' Whether we like it or not, differences exist. To punish, revile and reject those people who don't fit our standard of what's 'normal' is cruel and deeply hurtful. I do know and understand that not all share my point of view on this. I respect that this is their right.

Not that long ago, I saw a video on CNN entitled, *When your young daughter says "I'm a boy," Raising Ryland: the story of a young transgender child* by Kelly Wallace. It was about a couple whose son was transgender (currently referred to as absent "gender conformity") at a very early age. The mother made the comment that with the attempted suicide rate at forty-one percent, she'd "rather have a living son than a dead daughter." Gender identity is something in your sense of self and mind—who you are authentically as opposed to your anatomy. When those elements are out of sync with each other, then physical gender and authentic self are mismatched. After their son's statement at age four that maybe when the family dies he could cut his hair, the parents were able to let go of the last traces (hair and bows) of their daughter and fully embrace their son.

This subject was portrayed in the movie, *The Danish Girl*, based on the fictional novel by David Ebershoff by the same name, and inspired by the life of Lili Elbe, one of the first people to have gender reassignment surgery.

Asking the question of "Why a man would *choose* to be gay?" is a deliberate effort to debunk the mythology and belief held by some that being gay is a choice. Who we are attracted to romantically and sexually just *is*, much like feelings. Do heterosexuals 'choose' to be straight? Think about that one, if you never have. By referring to men, I don't at all mean to suggest that it is easier for women, as I know they face their own version of judgment, ostracism, negative comments and the like. In some school districts in states like Texas, where I live, a lesbian risks losing her job if she is 'out' in her work environment. The path is not an easy one. In the movie *Carol,* the even more difficult path for lesbians in the past was portrayed in a loving, yet heartbreaking manner. The movie was based on the book, originally with a different title and written under a pseudonym (after being rejected by the author's already established publisher), later republished as *Carol,* still with a pseudonym in 1952, then finally, at long last, as *Carol* by Patricia Highsmith, (the author's real name) in 1990. If we look at the trajectory over time, it becomes clear that the stages of acceptance spanned over forty years. That fact speaks volumes.

Being bisexual brings its own set of problems. Often they lack a sense of belonging in any world-gay or straight, which may subject them to prejudice and exclusion, leaving them nowhere to fit in except with other bisexuals. That narrows the support pool and can make finding a partner very challenging.

 The news is replete with articles and stories about teenagers who have been shamed and bullied about their sexual orientation to the point of suicide. The word 'gay' is still used in a pejorative fashion, even when it doesn't relate to sexual orientation.

The newest acronym encompassing all areas of sexuality excluding heterosexuals is LGBTQ. The addition of the Q makes the acronym more all-inclusive. It stands for Lesbian, Gay, Bisexual, Transgender and Queer or Questioning. Another word gaining common use in my field is 'cisgender', for a person whose gender identity corresponds with their biological birth gender. For some this will be a stretch; for others it creates a level playing field around the subject of gender identity.

Most, if not all, gay men have a sense of unease or guardedness much of the time, which can quickly turn to fear under the right circumstances. I am reminded of the things I've learned about African American slavery and its subsequent holdover. Feeling unsafe in the world you live in is something no one deserves. Black lives matter. In no way do I mean to detract from that by saying all lives matter. The more our consciousness is raised and our ability not only to tolerate, but, ideally, embrace diversity of all kinds, the more likely it becomes that this will be true someday. There must be room for all of us, no matter our religion, race, nationality, sexual orientation, etc. to live in a safe and peaceful world. Embracing diversity is our best hope for that outcome.

Sexual Abuse

I regret that I am not able to address this important and difficult topic in more depth. I am grateful for the excellent work of others on this subject, so readers have many resources for information on this and any other topic.

I've worked with a great many adult survivors of childhood sexual abuse over many years, and it has devastating, far-reaching negative consequences. When a child is sexually molested, it not only causes great emotional (and sometimes physical) harm, it interrupts the natural development of a healthy sense of sexuality, body image, trust and safety. The damage is inestimable. This does not mean that recovery and healing are impossible. It's a long, difficult and often painful road to travel, but well worth it to come out on the other side. Although many books have been written on this subject, the seminal work is *The Courage to Heal: A Guide for Women Survivors of Child Sexual Abuse* by Ellen Bass and Laura Davis. As noted in the title, it was written for women. But, when it was written in 1988 people were in the early stages of recognition and acknowledgment that sexual abuse of children occurred. Even less frequently recognized or attended to was the fact that this happened to boys, as well as girls. With movies such as *Spotlight* (so aptly named) we can see how much that has changed.

Bass and Davis have written many subsequent books on related topics, including a workbook for survivors, a book for partners of survivors and one for LGBT children. The following are some quotes from women at the beginning of their first watershed book: "*The Courage to Heal* touched the deepest part of me, the part that has been walled off and silent for 25 years. You have spoken the words for me that I was unable to utter." "When your book entered my life, it gave me the reassurance that one day I would be whole." "Dealing with feelings that have been hidden, suppressed and unacknowledged for fifty years is an awesome task, and your book is helping to make the process bearable and possible." These quotes are a testament to the power of the work.

I'm not sure where I first heard the expression, "Thrive, don't merely survive," but it has resonated with me in a very important way. Although survival is essential, thriving is optimum. For those who have suffered any kind of abuse, it can only be healed if it is talked about, worked through and resolved to the point where it no longer interferes with your life and your happiness. This is not reserved for sexual abuse, but applies to survivors of any kind. Surviving trauma, loss, illness, etc. takes courage and fortitude. As so aptly stated in the book's title, healing requires courage.

Another documentary film on the subject of campus rape in the United States, *The Hunting Ground* dealt with institutional cover-ups and the devastating effect upon the students and their families. Although no longer 'technically' children, most college age students are not fully adult, either. They are adolescents, so they mostly fall more into the category of children. The focus on this problem is important, and the documentary movie was well received, as was its theme song nominated for best original song at the 88th Academy Awards, co-written and performed by Lady Gaga at the Oscars, *Til It Happens to You*. Adult sexual abuse is somewhat different, although abuse is abuse. Rape or any other forced sexual act which is not consensual constitutes abuse and is traumatic, no matter when or at what age it occurs. Trauma and its common aftermath PTSD (Post Traumatic Stress Disorder) require resolution, which is most often accomplished with therapy.

● ● ●

Expanding Us

When Becoming a Parent isn't as Easy as 1-2-3

Having gone through four years of not being able to become pregnant, it was no surprise when I decided to write my master's thesis on the psychosocial aspects of infertility. As fate would have it, I finished typing the thesis the day before I went into labor with my first son. My second pregnancy ended with a stillborn baby daughter, painfully furthering my understanding of all the loss infertility entails. Happily, my third pregnancy resulted in a very premature, but eventually healthy son. After I had sufficient time to heal my losses, I specialized in this area and saw many couples and individuals going through some kind of loss around having or attempting to have children. I led a support group for heterosexual couples dealing with infertility, which was very helpful to the women, but I think especially so for the men. I cannot write this book without including this topic. It embodies loss, potential assault to self-esteem, a sense of isolation in society and even in family, an artificiality of the natural ebb and flow of sexual desire, and a possible rift in a couple's relationship. It also embodies hope and may represent an end result of becoming a parent through whatever avenue, discovery of family and friends as a wonderful support system, and a shared bond and closeness between the couple due to their shared experience. Unless the couple resolves infertility by deciding not to become parents, which is a viable choice, there is a very deep level of appreciation for the child, because of the growth that is heightened by what came before.

One of the things that makes infertility so painful and difficult is that it is so abstract. I have been saying for years that, until Hallmark comes out with a card acknowledging how painful a loss this experience is, it will remain something that is usually not talked about. The custom to not share news of a pregnancy until after the first trimester can increase and intensify the sense of isolation after early miscarriage. Some mental health professionals, as well as those less schooled in the area of loss say some very hurtful things to people in their effort to help them. I've heard quotes such as "it's been three months since your miscarriage, it's time to move on." "It wasn't meant to be," etc. None of that is comforting. When I was writing my thesis, thirty-eight years ago, only one book had been published about infertility with one more in the process of being written. Although I admit it did make my literature review section quite easy, it wasn't worth the trade-off.

When people experience infertility, whether it be the inability to become pregnant, the inability to carry a pregnancy to term, or newborn loss, it has a devastating emotional impact. Most often, when people come to see me for this reason, they have not shared this information with any or many people in their lives. Keeping this information private exacerbates the level of pain. The couple has only each other to turn to. This, as well as the medical process of assisted reproductive technology, can put a tremendous strain on the couple's relationship. True to gender, women usually want to talk about it—a lot. And stereotypically, men much less so. This is a good example of how and why it rarely works to put all our needs in our spouse's 'basket.' In addition, people who are struggling with infertility often feel badly about themselves or guilty toward their partner. Sometimes it's a mixed blessing when both partners have some sort of contributing problem. It evens the playing field despite adding to the hurdles. There is a tremendously helpful support group called RESOLVE. Like any adversity, this experience can draw couples closer or create distance. It is rare that infertility does not wreak havoc with a couple's sexual relationship. Sex on demand for reproductive purposes over a long period of time does not make for many enjoyable experiences. Fortunately, many books now exist to help people through this process.

Now Let's Add the Kids

Before I had children, I remember being told that my life would change completely once I had a child. However, I had no idea the breadth of that change until it actually happened. My first conscious awareness was when I was halfway out the door to mail a letter at the post office, and was brought up short to realize that I had almost just left my infant son home alone! Esther Perel has made the observation that for the first eighteen months of a child's life, a woman's passion is directed toward the child and being a good parent. Although the number of months is arbitrary, I do believe this is a good 'guestimate.' Her point is that the woman's passion has not disappeared, it has merely been redirected. I think this would be a great thing for parents to learn before they have children. So often, men feel displaced by the arrival of the child, even though they may welcome the arrival with open arms. For a woman, it is a complex time. Assuming she carried the child during their pregnancy, her body has been shared for many months with the baby. This is a very intimate and intense experience. From the time she begins to think about conception, she is keenly aware of what she eats, drinks, and allows herself to be exposed to. When a pregnant woman first feels movement inside her, it is a miraculous and wondrous experience. Her awareness of the infant is heightened greatly. She is literally carrying precious cargo.

Once the child is born, if she is breastfeeding, her body continues to serve the function of sustaining her child's life, including hormonal changes that will likely dampen her sex drive. The psychological impact of a pregnancy and a nursing mother is tremendous.

When postpartum depression occurs, as it does with some mothers, it exceeds the more common 'baby blues' and may include mood swings, crying spells, anxiety, sleep difficulties, etc. Baby blues most often occur within the first few days after delivery and can last for a couple of weeks. However, some new mothers experience a more severe and longer lasting form of depression and/or anxiety, which is a psychological complication of giving birth. Prompt treatment to help manage symptoms is needed. Sometimes women feel there is something wrong with them for feeling depressed or anxious—after all, isn't this supposed to be a joyful time? By judging themselves this way, they often extend this difficult situation by neglecting to seek the help they need. Partners who are supportive and encourage the mother's self-care can be of tremendous help.

Men have some suspicion of what this entire 'having a baby' process is about, however they clearly can't experience it firsthand. Going back for a moment to the subject of women's power, adult men are once again reminded of this when women become mothers. This is no less true when a child is adopted. It is not necessary to experience a pregnancy or to nurse a child in order to become a mother or a father. Once a child arrives and is yours, the manner in which the child arrived becomes a whole lot less significant than the existence of the child.

Whether a child enters the couple's life through pregnancy or adoption, changes will occur. I recently heard a biological mother say to an adoptive mother, "I didn't feel like a mother until I held my baby in my arms." The adoptive mother replied, "Neither did I." Not everyone adopts babies, but everyone who adopts becomes a parent. A further note here about bonding: once again, parents are often quick to judge themselves if the bonding process isn't instantaneous. Bonding may be instant, but often occurs over a period of days, weeks, months and it may even take years to be fully bonded with a child. There's no right way-it just happens when it happens.

When it comes to sexuality, there may be some distinct differences. I believe it's difficult for many women to shift back and forth between the role of mother and wife, provider of sustenance to a baby and the freedom to experience their bodies in a sexual way, as well. Women want to keep the boundaries clear between motherhood and sexuality. Sometimes they struggle with this during pregnancy, sometimes while nursing, and sometimes not at all. It depends upon the woman, and each is unique and individual. I do, however, believe it is important for both women and men to be aware of this possible dichotomy and its source. I believe men feel less displaced if they understand what is going on with their female partner, and women have more clarity about themselves if in fact, that's the case.

Now the couple has become a family of three or more. At the beginning, the focus shifts. It is all about the baby or babies. This is a very special time in people's lives, and most of us with children wouldn't want it any other way. But what happens when the focus stays on the child and doesn't revert to a combination of the child or children and partner? In other words, the couple loses their connection in favor of the child.

This is where I often see problems. We live in a child-centered culture. Adding children into the mix complicates things considerably. Having children does not necessarily help a marriage. That said, parenthood is both a challenge to a couple's relationship and a potentially enriching component—much like adding the 'Us' to the 'Me.' It's how the couple handles life with children that really matters the most. Child-centered families cause many problems for not only the couple, but the children as well. Although in my generation, which takes us back to when children were to be 'seen and not heard,' we were guilty of the opposite extreme. Children were not necessarily treated with respect, and it was considered 'normal.' I believe children deserve and are worthy of respect. They are human beings from birth. Author Richard Carlson makes the statement in one of his book series, *Don't Sweat the Small Stuff, with Your Family*, "THINK IN TERMS OF MY CHILD, MY TEACHER." That's a very different attitude and embodies respect. It's also true. We do learn from our children.

On the other hand, I do not believe that children are part of a democracy within the family. My view is that they are part of a family headed by the parents, and exist in what I like to call a 'benevolent dictatorship.' They are entitled to express their feelings in a respectful manner. If they are taught how to do this, their opinions and feelings will be duly considered by their parents. The final decision about everything, however, rests with the adults. All too often, I see families where few if any limits are set for the children. This is not good for the children or for the adults. Children need limits and do not fare well without them. We are tempted to err on the side of not damaging our children emotionally to the point that we sometimes damage them by not saying no. Good parenting means setting good limits and helping children contain emotions when they are out of control. We won't always be popular, and we might hear, "You're mean," more than we'd like. However, our children will benefit, and that is what's most important.

I think it's really hard to be rearing children today. I also think it's hard on the kids themselves, although they have no basis for comparison. I really wish I had the formula for how a family balances their children's activities along with school, social and family life. I do believe that the balance is necessary and oftentimes missing.

It's time to get back to the oxygen mask. I'm not meaning to give the impression that children are not both precious and important. That's something I certainly don't believe. However, I see so much sacrifice on the part of parents for themselves, as well as for the two of them as a couple, that the concepts of first me and then you seem to fall by the wayside. I have a great deal of respect for the generation taking it all on today. Much of my time in working with couples is spent focusing on how they can carve out time for themselves and for each other. This is especially challenging with babies and young children whose needs and wants supersede everything else. Nevertheless, to the best of their ability and to whatever extent possible, the individual parent and the couple require attention in order to fare well. Once benign neglect has set in and taken its toll, they are in danger of losing themselves or parts of themselves, along with the risk of losing the emotional intimacy needed to sustain their relationship with each other.

This can be dangerous and create serious consequences for both parents and children. Not only is it important for the individuals and the couple relationship, but it's also damaging all around if one or both parents develop a primary relationship with a child in place of their relationship with their partner. The 'Then You' becomes a parent/child dyad, inherently unhealthy for all. It can be easy to fall into this trap, as we usually experience unconditional love from our kids (at least until they get older), whereas our partners are much more aware of our flaws and at least on occasion, more likely to point them out to us. In addition to losing that close connection with our partner, we create a dilemma for our child. It is an important developmental step for children to accept that mommy or daddy is already taken, so they can move on to find their own partner when old enough to do so. Despite the fact that most children wish for the undivided attention of their parents, receiving top priority casts them in an adult role and sets them up for attachment difficulty with romantic significant others if no one else can ever live up to that 'perfect parent' and if they have not detached in that necessary way from their parent. In instances where their parents' marriage ends, they will feel intensely displaced by a new partner who may almost literally 'steal' their parent away. These are only some scenarios that can culminate from this inherently unhealthy situation. Keep clear that you come first, and that your partner comes second. The kids, unless it's mandated otherwise by circumstances, come third.

Often I hear couples saying they shouldn't have to schedule date night, me time, sex, etc. I point out to them that when they were dating they scheduled everything. Just because you live with someone doesn't mean that things are going to spontaneously occur, especially once there are children in the picture. Once again, it would be so wonderful if someone had taught us all of this, yet in most cases, no one did.

Great news, though, when it comes to child-rearing: although not all parents who are still raising their kids know this, there are actually books! Many people don't know that with each developmental stage of childhood, a reciprocal parenting change must occur. It's back to the deep end of the pool without floaties, let alone lessons. I recommend the *On Becoming* series of (so far) eight books by Gary Ezzo, M.A. and Robert Bucknam, M.D, the latest of which is *On becoming baby wise: Giving your infant the GIFT of nighttime sleep.* Their books cover all the different stages of development from babyhood to teens. Since we can't parent our toddlers the same way we do infants, our kindergarteners the way we do our toddlers, junior high, high school, etc., the parenting must shift along with the developmental stage of the children. This has been broken down into the following stages in *On Becoming* books: infancy; 5-12 months; 12-18 months; 3-7 year olds; 8-12 year olds; preteens and teens. And to think that my generation of parents only had Dr. Spock! I very much wish I'd had these when I was raising kids. I'm so happy parents and children have these resources today, not to mention the movie *Inside Out,* about which it was a toss-up as to whether my granddaughter or I enjoyed it the most. What an amazing job of portraying and illustrating feelings to young children! This movie represents a breakthrough of magnitude, which goes hand-in-glove with the wonderful children's programming on television, also addressing feelings and relationships. There are a number of good books written to help parents with the joys and challenges of raising kids, and the Internet will be happy to lead the way. Changing our parenting doesn't mean parents can't continue to adopt the same parenting style as far as values, rules, consequences, etc., but the delivery, as well as the content must be fluid in order to meet our children 'where they're at.' The shift at adolescence is one that can't be ignored, or if it is, neither the adolescent nor the parents will fare well. Not only is it necessary to make changes in parenting along with developmental changes, it is also important to recognize what type of parenting each individual child responds to best. This is one of the three most difficult things we must do in life for which we are rarely prepared. I believe the word 'coasting' and the concept of 'flying by the seat of one's pants' are often quite apt, although now there are greater resources available to those who seek them.

From the book *On Becoming Preteen Wise: Parenting Your Child from 8 to 12 Years*, Ezzo and Bucknam state that there is a dearth of information regarding children's middle years, and write: "One possible explanation lies in the character of our society, which seems very willing to spend time and money to fix its problems, but very little of either to prevent them." They go on to say, "When we are in a crisis, we have incredible resolve to find solutions for problems. If we had the same resolve to prevent those crises, we might avoid many trials and much pain." I believe these words of wisdom apply to much more than just parenting. Preventing the problems would entail educating, and I believe we are sorely lacking in this regard. Dr. Bucknam continues with the following, "The 1500 days of preadolescence are all the time you have to prepare your kids for the nearly 3700 days of adolescence. Let's make the most of every minute." Our children grow up so very quickly. Let's cherish those precious moments we have with them.

Adolescence is 'the terrible twos' part two. On steroids. When our kids are toddlers, we have more of an ability to contain them and deal with them with a much more hands-on approach. As adolescents, we have far less ability to witness many of the things our kids are doing, since they have so much more autonomy and are not around us all or even most of the time. It doesn't help when we remember some of the more outrageous or downright dangerous exploits from our own lives during those same ages. We know we're entitled to be worried!

From the standpoint of our adolescent children, we are as out of touch as we perceived our own parents to be. They may or may not turn to us for guidance, but most often they will not welcome our input or advice with open arms (despite the fact they may follow it behind our backs). This is where the immortal words of Mark Twain come to mind: *"When I was a boy of 14, my father was so ignorant I could hardly stand to have the old man around. But when I got to be 21, I was astonished at how much the old man had learned in seven years."*

When we reach adolescence, merely having a parent can be an embarrassment. We would prefer (for the most part) that our parents be invisible among our peers. If they must show themselves for purposes such as driving us places, it's best if they don't speak or even breathe too loudly. Sometimes that's a real 'owwie' for parents. I always encourage them not to take this or the abrupt ceasing of public displays of affection personally. It's all part of the process. An excruciating self-awareness emerges in adolescence, and it is a time of major emotional imprinting. Adolescents are trying to figure out where they fit in everywhere in their world. Since they haven't fully left childhood nor fully achieved adulthood, it's a no-man's-land in almost every space they inhabit—home, school, socially, etc. Being an individual at this stage is tough, for anyone. This is the first time they are really assessing themselves in some version of an adult form, and being different is anathema. Just as they want their parents invisible, they sometimes also wish that for themselves. Achievement recognition might generally be a good way to stand out for most pre-teens and teens, however not always and not for all. No one ever wants to stand out in a negative way—ever.

● ● ●

Before we leave the section on families, including helpful books, I must mention one certain to bring 'comic relief' and probably a lot more. In his extremely humorous book, *I Am America (And So Can You!)*, Stephen Colbert, host of *The Late Show*, formerly of *The Colbert Report*, does a wonderful counterpoint to many of the same topics I'm addressing. His irreverent and highly intelligent wit frequently has me laughing so hard I lose my ability to speak. If you haven't discovered him yet, I encourage you to. Colbert's outrageous suggestions range from the mildly absurd to the hilarious extreme. Just as I see crying as hydrotherapy, I do believe that laughter *is* the best medicine!

Balancing Parenthood and Sexuality

The statistics on marital satisfaction after children indicate a decline. This doesn't mean it's true for every marriage, as common as it is. Now that same sex marriage has become legal, we may well be talking about either gender in either role. Women may have conflicts about their dual roles after giving birth, and their partners can feel displaced. Now that many men take a much more active role in parenting, it's likely that those satisfaction statistics may change over time for hetero couples. One of the things I ask couples with small children is, "Who is in bed first every night?" The most common answer is the parent who is not the primary caregiver for the children. When I probe further and ask what the person who is not in bed (let's say the 'mother') is doing, it is generally either chores related to the home or children or (and this one is less likely) taking some time for themselves after completing those chores. I ask whether the partner would be willing to help so that they might both be able to go to bed at the same time. Most of the time, they are able to work this out. There are cases, however, where one partner sees necessity where the other partner sees excess. Then it becomes a matter of negotiation and choice. For example, Alicia wanted to have the house perfectly clean and everything in its place before she could comfortably go to bed. Her husband, Blake, thought this was overkill. He didn't mind helping up to a point, but he wanted some time for himself, as well as with his wife. In their discussion of this dilemma, Blake asked Alicia if she thought she could settle for less in terms of the house being in perfect condition every night. He told her he'd be happy to help out more in exchange for her doing less. Alicia came to the conclusion that she had become enslaved to the notion of being a good housekeeper at the expense of her own individual time and time with her husband. Together they made a list of necessary tasks, their division, and how and when each wanted to spend their time alone and together. This didn't happen overnight, but they kept at it until both were satisfied.

Many couples report change in their sexual history after children. Part of the explanation for this may have something to do with the fact that sexual desire is often facilitated by regularity. The rhythm of sexual activity frequently declines during and after pregnancy, so the pattern changes. It's also often the case that there is a 'need for speed' in lovemaking, which may impact the quality. A woman's view of herself as a mother can complicate her sexual identity. It can also change how a man sees a woman. She may seem less sexy and be more exhausted, and he may have some difficulty adjusting to her as both a mother and a sexual partner. This is particularly present in what is known as the Madonna/Whore syndrome, although this division can exist without the presence of children. Basically, it means that a man can see a woman as a sexual being only if she is not his wife and (once again, it can be either or both) the mother of his children. This division between 'good girls' and 'bad girls' is probably less common now than in the past; however, it still exists in some cases. It's a complex situation with individual variations.

Looking at the positives, and there can be many, women often feel empowered by pregnancy, nursing and motherhood (however the last comes about) in a way they never experienced before. The fact that a woman's body can contain, grow and sustain another human life is awe inspiring. Many women flourish while pregnant, despite some of the inconveniences. Even with the fatigue they often experience in early and late pregnancy, they may find a significant energy surge at times, especially in the middle of pregnancy. Having a baby may not only give a woman greater confidence in what she's capable of (not just the pregnancy, but the continued tending to and sustaining the life and well-being of her child), but greater confidence in her body, as well. For some women, the pressure to be physically perfect is lifted, and they can more fully enjoy their sexuality. To be a mother is no longer seen as a diminution in sex appeal and seeing themselves as sexually desirable is a very positive thing for most women. Many men can fall in love all over again with their wives when they become mothers, enhancing their beauty as a woman, not just a 'hot chick.'

For the men, there are also positive benefits. They find a new way to love, as do the women—for the love of one's child is different than any other. Having their hearts opened to this 'new love' is a wonderful gift for them. Men feel tenderness, protectiveness, increased patience, and a whole array of feelings previously either not experienced or perhaps reserved for a very few. Their new role not only increases their emotional realm, it can make them feel more of a man—a father, as well as all the other aspects of manhood. For the couple, seeing these changes in each other creates a whole new perspective of their partner. Oh, and I don't want to leave out the joy. Having children, and having the opportunity to see them grow and discover from the simple things to the more complex, allows us a never before experienced view of the world according to them, and an endless supply of joy in their love and 'becoming.'

Roles, expectations, division of labor, working outside the home and so on, are factors which effect feelings about oneself, as well as one's partner. In addition, both partners have to make major changes at a difficult time, i.e. the addition of a child. Mothers may find themselves insecure about the changes in their appearance, for example additional weight after pregnancy or changes in their bodies, and may experience their husbands as being more interested in the baby than them. Fathers may feel displaced and experience their wives as focusing only on the child and not them. As mentioned before, fathers may also have some difficulty adjusting to their wife's role as both a mother and as the focus of his sexual interest. It's important that he be able to separate those aspects of her, as well. However, the opposite of being less important or drawn away may occur for both mom and dad. Couples who work as a team have higher marital satisfaction and a generally easier time of things because it is, after all, a joint venture and adventure!

● ● ●

Challenges to 'Happily Ever After'

Abuse

Abuse can be subtle, insidious, difficult to define, or overt. Much like child abuse, it is often hard to spot. So many times with caution, I've actually had to ask someone if they thought they were being abused. Sometimes they say yes. Often, they say, "No" or "I'm not sure." This is not only true for women, but often especially so for men. The notion that a woman is abusing them, especially physically, seems patently absurd. After all, women are the 'weaker sex.' But this thinking is wrong. Women are capable of harming men, with or without a physical weapon.

Sometimes the easiest way to get in touch with abuse is to get in touch with how you are feeling in relation to your partner. Physical abuse is easiest to spot and is the most flagrant form. This is where boundaries come in and become so important. If someone will not let you be alone when you ask for time out, physically blocks your ability to leave or get past them, grabs you to hold you in place, pushes, hits, kicks, punches or touches you in any way which is unacceptable to you, this constitutes abuse. It is a violation of boundaries and causes distress. It sometimes results in injuries and often creates fear. Rape or any forced sexual activity is abuse and is traumatic. There are those who think if they are a couple or are married, it doesn't constitute abuse. It most certainly does.

Violation of any boundaries, whether those violations are verbal, emotional or physical are abusive. Name-calling, put downs, hitting below the belt (using something against someone that the other person knows is a vulnerability for them) all constitute abuse. I'm not interested in labeling, but I am interested in mutual respect, self-protection and safety--both physical and emotional.

When abuse occurs in a couple's relationship, it generally isn't seen as abuse by the one (unless both are being abusive) who isn't feeling fearful and unsafe. Many people assume that men are always the abusers and women always the victims. This is definitely not the case. I've seen men who were emotionally, verbally and physically battered by their female partners. The person in the role of abuser generally feels guilty and ashamed after they have done something harmful to their partner. If they don't have these feelings of remorse, it either means they're in denial about the damage they cause, or they're sociopaths, incapable of feeling empathy or guilt. The former group, with some help, is usually able to see and break through the denial so that they can own their behavior and make efforts to change it. Sociopaths don't have this capacity. A word of caution: just because someone may not know their partner has remorse doesn't mean they don't. If a diagnosis must be made, I urge people to allow a trained, licensed and impartial professional to be the one to do it.

Looking at the person who is the recipient of abuse, denial often plays a role. "He didn't really mean it," "I'm just being too sensitive," "She has so much stress at work or at home with the children," etc. Excuses are made. It's hard to face something that may be a threat to a valued relationship. Although this is very understandable, it is also a very destructive pattern for all involved. Children learn from their parents what the roles of father, mother, husband and wife look like. In these instances, the parents are modeling very dysfunctional roles which the children may be likely to replicate.

Sometimes talking about the impact on their children is the only way I can reach the parent. As I said, this is a difficult thing to confront, because it can very much threaten the existence of the relationship once acknowledged. When abuse is occurring, either or both partners do not feel safe emotionally and/or physically. Safety is an essential, primary need for functioning in a healthy way. The expression I most often hear is "walking on eggshells." I submit this is no way to live.

Fortunately, this can be changed. It does involve the awareness, ownership, cooperation and willingness to change for both partners. The abused partner plays a role and has responsibility for accepting ill-treatment. Sometimes there is reciprocal abuse; the original recipient justifying their behavior as fighting back. Very often in this instance they see themselves as a victim, and they may be. Although there may be truth to that contention, their willingness to stay in that role or inability to step out of it represents their part of the equation; however, in severe instances there may be real and present danger which pose a tremendous risk in leaving, both to the spouse and to their children. It's certainly being caught between a rock and a hard place; however, continuing to tolerate abuse or bear witness to child abuse and failing to protect their child and themselves is a lose/lose for all. Despite the feelings of powerlessness and potential risk, it is ultimately better to leave than to stay. Very often an unprotected child feels more anger toward the parent who failed to protect than the one who abused them. The one who didn't abuse them was the one they counted on for help.

I always tell couples they can't take more than fifty percent of the credit in a relationship. This is because there are two people involved. We each have the ability to self-determine what we are willing or able to do in relation to our partner.

In order to break the cycle of abuse, it is usually necessary to seek outside professional help. If the abuse is extreme, leaving may be necessary, as well as calling the police. This is something that people are almost always either afraid or very reluctant to do. It's important that they understand that if they are powerless against their partner in a physical way, calling the police is the only viable alternative. I also suggest that they be prepared with an exit strategy at all times. This might mean having a bag packed to leave for the night, making sure they have cab money when they go out, driving in separate cars, etc. There's nothing worse than feeling imprisoned and forced to endure abuse. In cases where there is danger in leaving, this is, of course, much more difficult. We see instances in the news that are frightening and reinforce the notion that staying is the only available option. It's easy for me to say there are shelters where people can stay in safety and anonymity; however, I do understand there's no 'witness protection' for them. The stakes are high. In my opinion, they're high either way.

No one deserves to be abused under any circumstances, and everyone deserves to stand up for themselves and to protect themselves or to have a parent protect them. This is one of those rare black and white things which actually exist in a gray world. It doesn't matter if one's partner doesn't agree that abuse is occurring, for it only takes one to define their own reality. If the partner who feels abused is out of touch with reality, i.e. mentally ill, that might constitute an exception; however, this is not the population to whom I am speaking. Protecting yourself or seeking help for protection is not only your right, but your *responsibility* if you're taking care of yourself and your children.

Affairs

When a woman or a man has an affair and leaves their marriage, they are not leaving for the other person, they are leaving for themselves. People always leave for themselves, whether or not there is a third party involved. The left spouse is often tormented by thoughts of what they did wrong, what this other person has to offer which is better than what they offered, and so on, ad infinitum. The simple truth—things were not working well enough (usually for both parties, but one may have been in denial or simply unaware), and the one who let themselves know that fact actually left for themselves.

Although this can be a difficult concept to embrace, sometimes when affairs occur they are an unconscious effort to help the marriage. I understand that this can be difficult to conceptualize, especially for the one who didn't have the affair. An affair stirs things up in a marriage. There are a multitude of reasons why people, even those in happy relationships may be unfaithful. This idea is addressed in the TED Talk, Esther Perel: Rethinking infidelity...a talk for anyone who has ever loved. Perel states that affairs, often seen as something wrong with the one who cheats or with the relationship, may very well be neither. She cites things such as "an expression of longing and loss: longing for a sense of aliveness, emotional connection, novelty, freedom, and as an outgrowth of loss or awareness of mortality," to name only some of the many possibilities for affairs. Perel's point is that the person who strays isn't always looking for another person as much as another self (or version of themselves).

She also introduces a very constructive concept about being investigative about what it was like for the person who had the affair—"what did they feel, what was there with the other that wasn't there with their relationship, and what do they value about their own relationship?" She encourages this as opposed to the usual interrogation about all the details of the affair, which only serves to inflict more pain. She states that it's vitally important that the person who was unfaithful take responsibility for their actions and acknowledge and express guilt and remorse for hurting their partner, even if they don't feel guilt and remorse about the experience of the affair itself. If they will be the one to bring the subject up, it will potentially relieve their partner from obsessing about it by having it out in the open. Perel, an astute observer of human behaviors and the broad spectrum of motivations behind them, says that most of us will have two or three marriages in our lifetimes. "The question is whether or not we want to have them with the same person." The old marriage is over after an affair, she states. Sometimes the threat of loss and the opening of communication can bring a similar vitality and imagination found in the affair into the 'new' marriage. This catalyst makes many things possible in creating a more fulfilling and better order in the new one. I have seen this occur on many occasions.

On the other hand, sometimes affairs occur because one partner is unhappy and either has given up or doesn't know how to make things better. They may need to have a replacement before they can leave the marriage. I highly recommend Janis Abrahms Spring's, *After the Affair: Healing the Pain and Rebuilding Trust When a Partner Has Been Unfaithful Completely Updated Second Edition* and her subsequent book about forgiveness, *How Can I Forgive You: The Courage To Forgive, The Freedom Not To.* I'm looking forward to seeing a book from Esther Perel on affairs, as I know it will be wonderfully helpful and illuminating.

Some thoughts about forgiveness and grudges are worth stating here, not only as they refer to affairs, but in any applicable situation. In her book on forgiveness, Spring references something she calls 'cheap' forgiveness. This is given when a person believes (usually because that is what they were taught) that it is right to forgive, but doesn't actually forgive. Most people believe that the quote "To err is human; to forgive, divine," is biblical in origin. In fact, it was English poet Alexander Pope who, in a poem entitled *An Essay on Criticism, Part II* actually penned those words.

Equally interesting, two other well-known sayings come from the same poem: "A little learning is a dangerous thing" and "Fools rush in where angels fear to tread." Not only was Pope brilliant (how many common usage quotes stand up over such an extended period of time—1711?), but he certainly seems to have had a relationship with the heavens above, which is likely why most of us think biblical when we hear words like 'divine' and 'angels!'

Cindy came to therapy because she was finding it impossible to let go of an affair Bob had early in their relationship, but before their marriage. She found herself obsessing over it, especially the fact that he hadn't told her about it until after their marriage. Since Cindy tended toward obsessive thinking, it was a particularly difficult thing for her to let go. She couldn't forgive him, despite his zealous efforts to earn her forgiveness. I asked her if she was comfortable bringing Bob in with her. I suspect there was a small glimmer of hope on her part that I would take her side against him. I don't do that, nor did I think it would have advanced her progress had I been so inclined. For the record, I'm on the 'side' of the entity which is the couple when working with one. I don't choose one or the other person who comprise the couple to 'side' with.

Upon meeting Bob, I discovered that keeping the secret had been difficult for him. It became clear that Cindy was using the former affair to punish Bob, as well as a way to feel some control to protect herself from more hurt . Bob believed that if he would continue to tolerate what was now amounting to emotional and verbal abuse, Cindy would finally realize how much he loved her and forgive him. He was set upon proving this by allowing this behavior to continue forever, if necessary. Lest it seem that all my examples have happy endings, let me say that I attempted to reinforce that Cindy's behavior was unacceptable and that Bob deserved better treatment and a stronger sense of self-worth. I clarified that accepting Cindy's behavior in no way demonstrated how much he loved her, nor was it likely to convince her to forgive him. When they left therapy, this dynamic had lessened, but it had not ceased.

Obsessions cannot always be 'cured.' Forgiveness is not always granted even when earned. Tolerating abuse does not equate with loving. Having sufficient self-esteem takes time. And finally, not all therapy is successful!

Spring's subtitle *The Courage to Forgive: The Freedom Not To* speaks volumes. If forgiveness is not earned, we still have the freedom to accept and let go of the painful feelings associated with the injury. Holding grudges and dragging them out every time there is disagreement is a common occurrence in many couples' conflicts. This is not a functional or healthy way of disagreeing, in addition to the fact that the person who holds on to the past is continuing to live with that pain. Affairs are only one of many sources of pain and betrayal about which bringing up the past can occur.

Divorce

Obviously, affairs are far from being the only reason relationships end. In actuality more couples stay together after an affair, sometimes more happily, sometimes not. Perel makes the statement that staying with a partner after an affair is 'the new shame.' I've encountered this many times when a person feels they are weak, lacking in courage or in some other way, worried about others' perceptions of them, etc.

There are many forms of betrayal other than affairs, and sometimes marriages just settle into a pattern of stagnation or unease that may take time to acknowledge and address. My goal when working with couples is to help them find the answers they need to determine if they can be happy together or, if not, happy apart. If the couple is still invested in making the marriage work, I strive to help them attain that goal. If one or both has given up on the marriage, the goal then becomes how to pursue happiness apart from the marriage and to come apart in the least painful manner possible. Sometimes one partner wants to preserve the marriage, and the other is finished. In this case, there is only one possibility, which is to end the marriage, as it really does 'take two.'

In cases where the marriage is dissolved, it is so important and beneficial to separate in a way that is potentially healing, as opposed to destructive. This process is usually easier when there is no third party involvement, as emotions almost always run high in the face of that situation. Sometimes things must be dealt with as best they can. Since few, if any, marriages end on a happy note, but more often with a lot of hurt and anger, ending on a healing note may seem to be an impossible dream. That's why I advocate collaborative divorce. I trained in collaborative divorce as a mental health professional and was part of a study group comprised of attorneys, mental health professionals (or MHP's), and financial professionals. In collaborative law, each party has their own attorney with whom they sign a document stating that if they cannot come to an agreement about the terms of divorce, they will fire their lawyers and obtain new ones. This is a powerful incentive for both the attorneys and their clients to resolve differences and attain an agreement with which both parties can live. In addition to these four parties, there is a financial professional to help with those matters, and a mental health professional to ensure emotional safety and a healthy environment. Instead of battling it out in court, fighting over custody and finances, the framework is one of true collaboration. In this way, the couple retains control of the settlement agreement rather than handing it over to a judge, and the healing can begin during the process of ending the marriage. If I could mandate collaborative divorce as the new standard, I would definitely do so. Not all people are candidates for this type of resolution. Whenever possible, however, it is my strong recommendation.

Of the many books written about divorce, I often recommend (to both women and men, despite the fact that it was written for women) *Learning to Leave: A Woman's Guide* by Lynette Triere with Richard Peacock.

Blended Families

After a divorce or the death of a spouse, many people remarry. If one or both people in the new marriage have a child or children, they become a blended family (or stepfamily). Although this can be incredibly rewarding for all parties involved, it involves many challenges and complexities. When I began working with blended families, that term was a relatively new one, as opposed to the more familiar 'stepfamilies.' In 1982, I read what was then, to my knowledge, the only book written on the subject. On the cover of the book, *Stepfamilies: Myths and Realities*, by Emily B Visher, Ph.D. and John S. Visher, M.D., the authors were described as "producing a pioneering volume on professional work with stepfamilies." That seminal book was invaluable to mental health professionals and to people living in stepfamilies, as well. Fortunately since then, the Vishers and others have written many books on this topic. Being armed with knowledge is almost always an easier path than proceeding without knowing. For our purposes, I will use the divorce model here.

Blended families are all about change. Although change is something people may desire, it is not an easy thing to do. I would say that sums up blended families well. By definition, there are children involved. Remaining a devoted parent while prioritizing a new partner can be an exquisite exercise in diplomacy, not to mention an inevitable feeling of being caught in the middle. Sometimes, it seems impossible to please anyone. However, time does help, as does an understanding and supportive partner. In some ways, it is easier if both have a child, as there is the ability to relate to how challenging a task this is; however, it does complicate the equation. In that instance, both partners have to balance their biological children with the new relationships.

I often hear people say to their new partner, "If I have to choose, you know you'll lose." Although I understand their need to let their partner know how devoted they are as a parent, it can feel hurtful and alienating to hear this. It's better said, "I won't choose, so we will have to figure out a way to work it out together." I believe the first statement is fear-based. The goal is to make it abundantly clear not only to one's partner but also to reinforce to oneself, that the role of parent won't be sacrificed or abandoned in the face of this new relationship. This runs deep for almost any parent.

Assimilating to the new order is a process which takes time for all involved. The kids didn't pick this other person; they just got 'assigned.' Now having to share a parent when, before, the parent was single and had more time for them is an adjustment for any child. Having to live with a 'stranger' is also not often a welcomed experience. In addition, in the midst of all this, the children are likely grieving the loss of their original, intact family. Children need to find a balance between accepting their stepparent and loyalty to the same gender parent (especially if they sense that parent is feeling threatened by the new partner). In some instances, the other parent actively or unconsciously works to sabotage a connection between their children and this new person in their ex's life. They fear being displaced or being compared unfavorably. If there is disharmony and contention between the parents, this will heighten all aspects of the difficulty of the new family relationships. Kids do best when biological parents are able to put their differences aside when it comes to parenting and provide a cohesive co-parenting model for their children. The more this is the case, the more likely things will go smoothly.

Bringing cohesion to a step-family is a step by step process (pun definitely intended). Everyone involved needs time to get comfortable with and become accustomed to their new blended family. The relationship between stepchildren and stepparents requires time to grow and evolve. It's a trial and error, learn-as-you-go evolution. Expectations and assumptions are almost inevitable, so communication needs to be open and clear among all concerned. Often, stepparents assume they will be trusted. This is a risky assumption. Trust takes time to acquire and must be earned, no matter who the parties are. Trying to be a disciplinarian before the trust is well established will almost always cause problems. Giving it the necessary time is essential, and even then, "You're not my mother/father," will likely emerge. It's important, although difficult, not to take this personally. Kids are possibly just testing the limits, protecting their other parent or simply stating a fact. It's very important to communicate that the goal is not to replace their parent, but to be another adult in their life who cares about them and their well-being.

For the person who doesn't have a biological child of their own, this can be disappointing. There is sometimes a wish to fulfill that need within them if it exists. Part of the process is letting go of that dream and learning to embrace what *is* possible. Some people have a better relationship with their stepparent than with their biological parent. When this is the case, it often speaks to how well the stepparent is able to give without trying to displace the biological parent. Sometimes it's just an evolutionary stage, e.g. emotionally separating from the biological parent but feeling safer with the stepparent with whom the ties are not so complex. Many dynamics are involved in this not-so-simple framework.

When it comes to parenting decisions, limit setting, giving consequences, etc., it's important to recognize that the biological parent's vote may have to be deferred to by the stepparent. Conversely, it is important that the biological parent treats the stepparent with respect regarding their input and feelings, and that the two work as a team, providing a united front for the new family.

If we needed education about how to become a whole and happy person, a healthy couple and a good enough parent, we need at least as much, or more, instruction about how to create a harmonious outcome in a stepfamily. When it all comes together, the blended family experience has the potential to greatly enrich all the participants' lives. For people with no children of their own, it allows them to participate in parenting children whom they may very well grow to love. For those who are single parents, it affords them the opportunity to have a spouse who supports their parenting and provides a positive addition to the family. For children, it's getting a bit closer to that 'village' of which it's said it takes to raise a child. There are more people to potentially love and care for the children than just the two biological parents, and when that occurs, it's a very positive thing and cause for celebration.

Change

In 1971 David Bowie released the song *Changes*. In it, he referenced the difficulty of change. Not only is it difficult, it can be downright risky. Although I am a huge proponent for change when that change is for the better, I may often advise clients of the risks.

I've always found the definition of the word crisis to be very interesting. It is defined as 'an upset in a steady state.' According to that definition, as absurd as it may sound, a vacation fits the definition of a crisis. If you think about all that goes into a vacation, the planning, the arrangements, packing, the possible anxiety of making a plane on time, the possible anxiety about going to a new place for the first time, the return trip, unpacking, re-entry into life as usual, etc., you might begin to see how this qualifies as a crisis. Most would categorize a vacation as a positive thing. The fact that it fits the definition of a crisis does not take that away—most of the time it is a positive thing. It does, however, speak to the dual nature of change.

By no means do I want to discourage people from change endeavors; however, I do think a warning about the risks is warranted. In order to attain something positive, we often have to do so at a cost. Some examples of the risks of change can be seen in the treatment of depression. You only have to listen to the warnings attached to antidepressant medication on TV commercials or read them with the prescription itself to recognize this possibility. But even without medication, treatment for depression contains risks. In the process of working through painful issues, people sometimes become more depressed. This more severe depression may even represent a risk for self-injury or suicide. Although this outcome is thankfully not common, it does pose a risk for some.

I'm fond of saying that the only way I know to get to the other side is to go through. We would like to be able to go around, above or below in order to get there. None of that works. Change and growth require that we experience what's blocking it and learn to change behaviors, beliefs, and feelings. The term 'growing pains' can be aptly applied here.

Another aspect of change which people generally find frustrating is that it is not a steady progression upward or forward. It really is both baby steps, and one step forward, one step back. Sometimes it's one step forward, two steps back. When we've held on to something for many years, the effort to change it is going to take time. It is not, however, required that it takes as much time as it took to get to the place we're at. But it does take time and, as a result, patience and fortitude.

Sometimes people find this perplexing. If we want to change, why should it be so hard? At the risk of oversimplifying, it just is. We really would like to take the shortcut or the magic pill that doesn't exist, and that's because it is a difficult process. And the waiting is hard. If I didn't believe it was well worth the risk and hard work, I wouldn't espouse it. I do believe it's more than worth it!

There's a term used in psychology which I often share with my clients. It's called 'successive approximation.' It means simply that we are getting closer to our goal once we start moving in that direction and with each subsequent step we take. I believe that notion is helpful in keeping us going on our journey of change. If we don't break it down into the smaller parts, the whole idea of change can be overwhelming and daunting. If we don't understand that along the way we will slip back into old behaviors, patterns, thought processes, etc., we will easily become discouraged. We will want to throw in the towel. Perseverance is needed, as well as, you guessed it, courage.

Some years ago there were a slew of light bulb jokes and one of them involved therapy. It went like this: How many therapists does it take to change a light bulb? The answer? Only one, but it has to really want to change! I think that says it all.

When one person in a couple is in therapy by themselves, this can potentially cause a risk to the relationship. The reason for this is that if they are changing and growing but their partner is not, a gap between them may occur or, if already there, may widen. Conversely, it can have the opposite effect. When one partner changes, it usually will require their partner to change as well—if they are going to stay together and be in sync. The dance metaphor definitely applies here—it still takes two to tango!

If the partner not in therapy is open to change, then it may work very well. Because this outcome is unknown at the beginning, it is usually preferable that both partners be involved in therapy, at least to some extent. Harville Hendrix, author of *Getting the Love You Want* and other books, is a proponent of the theory that couples can serve as therapeutic agents in their relationships. I believe and have seen that this is quite possible.

* * *

"Being deeply loved by someone gives you strength, while loving someone deeply gives you courage."

— *Lao Tzu*

An Afterword

Happiness

Many of the things we learn, or don't have the opportunity to learn, interfere with our happiness, self-love and ability to have and maintain successful relationships. Happiness is an overall description of a feeling of well-being, of centeredness, of self-actualization, of peace, and of gratitude for all the good people and things in one's life. All of these are not always present, but they represent a 'go-to' place inside ourselves. When we have it, we have all the makings of a happy life. We are whole and complete. We love ourselves and treat ourselves well. We don't judge ourselves negatively. We work toward not judging others. We accept what is and those we love for whom they are. We surround ourselves (to the best of our ability to be in charge of that) with people who bring positive energy into our lives. We have hope and the capacity to look forward to the future, remember what we've learned from the past, and stay in the now so we can live our lives to the fullest.

● ● ●

My Wage

"I bargained with Life for a penny,
And Life would pay no more,
However I begged at evening
When I counted my scanty store.
For Life is a just employer.
He gives you what you ask.
But once you have set the wages,
Why, you must bear the task.
I worked for a menial's hire,
Only to learn, dismayed,
That any wage I had asked of Life,
Life would have willingly paid."

-Jessie B. Rittenhouse

Notes

Introduction

xi **Author Robert Fulghum**: Robert Fulghum. *All I Really Need to Know I Learned in Kindergarten: Reconsidered, Revised & Expanded with Twenty-five New Essays.* Random House Digital, Inc. 2003.

Preface

xiv **To quote Carl Rogers, founder of the humanistic psychology movement:** *Carl Rogers. On Becoming a Person.* Houghton Mifflin Harcourt Publishing Company. 1961.

xv **Maya Angelou on Courage:** Interview in *USA TODAY*. March 5, 1988.

Part 1: First Me

1 **Being Yourself**: Ralph Waldo Emerson. *Emerson: Essays and Lectures: Nature: Addresses and Lectures/Essays: First and Second Series/Representative.* Volume compilation, notes and chronology copyright 1983. Literary Classics of The United States, Inc. New York, New York. Penguin Putnam, Inc.

3 **Rousseau's scholarly explanations**: Jean-Jacques Rousseau. *Second Discourse.* Cambridge University Press, Cambridge. (1755 original copyright). 1997.

3 **Writer, teacher and entrepreneur Ozi Mizrahi wrote:** Osi Mizrahi. *The Importance of Loving Your Self.* Blog post October 2013. Retrieved from

http://www.huffingtonpost.com/osi-mizrahi/the-importance-of-loving-your-self_b_6196492.html

12 **The support organization:** ManKind Project Petitjean, P. 2006. *The Birth of the Scientific and Cultural History of Mankind Project. Sixty Years of Sciences at Unesco*, 1945-2005, 85-88.

12 **Support groups:** Alcoholics Anonymous and Al Anon

13 **A peek into therapy:** It's important that people feel they are talking to someone who is competent to help them and whom they can trust.

17 **British pediatrician and psychoanalyst Donald Winnicott's** "Good Enough Mother": Donald Winnicott. *The Maturational Process and the Facilitating Environment.* Hogarth Press. 1965.

21 **Stuart Smalley's affirmations resonated on television's Saturday Night Live**: Al Franken as Stuart Smalley. *I'm Good Enough, I'm Smart Enough, and Doggone it, People Like Me! Daily Affirmations by Stuart Smalley.* Dell Books. 1992.

22 **The movie from the Kathryn Stockett novel:** *The Help.* Tate Taylor. Writer & Director. Motion picture. Touchstone Pictures. 2011.

29 **More wisdom from Robert Fulghum**: Robert Fulghum. *All I Really Need to Know I Learned in Kindergarten: Reconsidered, Revised & Expanded with Twenty-five New Essays.* Random House Digital, Inc. 2003.

32 **The seminal work on child sexual abuse:** Ellen Bass and Laura Davis. *The Courage To Heal: A Guide For Women Survivors of Child Sexual Abuse.* Random House. 1988, 2002.

33 **The movie of the expose of priests' sexual abuse:** Anonymous Content et al. Tom McCarthy, Director & Co-writer. *Spotlight.* United States. Open Road Films. 2015.

34 **Writer John Irving:** John Irving. *The World According to Garp: a Novel.* Dutton. 1978.

34 **Television program:** *Kids Say the Darndest Things.* Hosted by Bill Cosby. CBS Production. 1998-2000.

36 **Author Flora Rheta Schreiber's non-fiction book:** Flora Rheta Schreiber. *Sybil.* Based upon psychoanalyst Cornelia B. Wilbur's treatment of a woman (Sybil is a pseudonym) for dissociative identity disorder. 1973. Vigil, L., & Martínez, S. (1981).

36 **Ego Psychology:** Based originally on Sigmund Freud's theory.

38 **Highly esteemed Swiss psychiatrist Carl Jung:** Carl Jung. *The Fight with the Shadow.* Listener, 7(7). 1946.

38 **Sir James Matthew Barrie was a Scottish novelist and playwright best known for Peter Pan:** James Matthew Barrie. *Peter Pan.* Hodder and Stoughton. 1911.

39 **Psychologist Harriet Goldhor Lerner writes on anger:** Harriet Goldhor Lerner. *The Dance of Anger: A Woman's Guide to Changing the Patterns of Intimate Relationships.* New York: Harper Collins. 1985.

40 **In her books on co-dependency Pia Mellody speaks of eight basic emotions:** Pia Mellody. *Breaking Free: A Recovery Handbook for "Facing Codependence".* Harper Collins. 1989.

40 **Psychologist, researcher and writer Brene Brown's TED Talk:** Brene Brown. *Listening to Shame.* [Video File]. 2012. Retrieved from https://www.ted.com/talks/brene_brown_listening_to_shame?language=en

40 **Researchers on the impact of Sesame Street:** Shalom M. Fisch, Rosemarie T. Truglio & Charlotte F. Cole. *The Impact of Sesame Street on Preschool Children: A Review and Synthesis of 30 Years' Research.* Media Psychology. 1(2), 165-190. 1999.

41 **At last, a wonderful movie about feelings:** *Inside Out.* Jonas Rivera. Producer. Pete Docter & Ronnie Del Carmen, Directors. Walt Disney Pixar Animation Studios. 2015.

44   **Psychologists George Bach & Herb Goldberg put a different spin on 'nice':** George Bach and Herb Goldberg. *Creative aggression: The Art of Assertive Living.* Wellness Institute, Inc. 1974.

47   **From the Broadway show:** *Guys and Dolls.* Frank Loesser. "Sit Down, You're Rockin' the Boat". Book by Abe Burrows & Jo Swerling. 1950.

47   **Helen Reddy proclaims:** Helen Reddy. "I Am Woman" on *I Don't Know How to Love Him.* [album] Capitol Records. 1970.

47   **Another musical roar from Katy Perry:** Katy Perry. "Roar" on *Prism.* [album] Capitol Records. 2013.

47   **Courage in song by:** Sarah Bareilles & Jack Antonoff. Sarah Bareilles. "Brave" on *The Blessed Unrest.* [album] Epic Records. 2013.

47   **From the movie Frozen:** Idina Menzel. "Let it Go." Kristen Anderson-Lopez & Robert Lopez composers. 2013.

50   **We are our own arbiters of truth:** Kelly Clarkson. "Catch My Breath" on *Greatest Hits — Chapter One.* [album] Co-writers Kelly Clarkson & Jason Halbert. Producers Jason Halbert & Eric Olson. RCA Records. 2012.

50   **Claiming our authenticity:** OneRepublic. "Counting Stars" on *Native* CD Single Digital download. Written by Ryan Tedder. Mosley-Interscope. 2013.

50   **Musically breaking rules:** X Ambassadors. "Renegades" on *VHS.* [album] KIDinaKORNER. Interscope. 2015.

52   **Abraham Maslow on Self-Actualization:** Abraham Maslow. *Some Basic Propositions of a Growth and Self-Actualization Psychology.* [Chapter in The Maslow Business Reader.] 31-53. 1962. 1958.

52   **Psychiatrist Kurt Goldstein who influenced Maslow:** Kurt Goldstein. *The Organism.* Zone Books. 1939.

52 **More on Maslow's Self-Actualization:** Abraham Maslow. *Lessons from the Peak-Experiences.* Article in The Journal of Humanistic Psychology. 1962.

53 **Maslow's biographer Edward Hoffman:** Edward Hoffman. *The right to be human: A biography of Abraham Maslow.* Jeremy P. Tarcher, Inc. 1988.

53 **Basic tenets as a guide to personal freedom and happiness:** Don Miguel Ruiz & Janet Mills. *The Four Agreements: A Practical Guide to Personal Freedom.* Amber-Allen Publishing. 2010.

54 **"Life is short, Break the rules...:** Mark Twain. Mark Twain & John S. Tuckey (Introduction). *The Devil's Race-Track.* University of California Press. 1876. Republished 1980.

Part 2: Then You

55 **Author unknown:** (attributed to Mark Twain)

59 **You're always 17...:** Cross Canadian Ragweed. "17" on *Cross Canadian Ragweed* [album]. Universal South. 2002.

63 **Save Yourself:** Beth Nielsen Chapman writer. *"Save Yourself."* Suzy Bogguss on *Aces* [album]. Liberty Records. 1991.

64 **About the teenage brain:** Daniel J. Siegel, M.D. *Brainstorm: The Power and Purpose of the Teenage Brain.* Penguin Group. 2014.

64 **Cool Kids:** Echosmith, Jeffrey David & Jesiah Dzwonek writers. "Cool Kids" on *Talking Dreams* [album]. Warner Brothers. 2014.

66 **"Love thy neighbor...:** "Love thy neighbor as thyself." The Old Testament. Leviticus 19:18. New International Version NIV.

68 **Susan Forward writes about the 'blinding FOG-fear obligation and guilt':** Susan Forward with Donna Frazier. *Emotional Blackmail: When the People in Your Life Use Fear,*

Obligation, and Guilt to Manipulate You. Harper Collins Publishers. 1998.

69   **Author John Lee writes on abandonment and regression:** John Lee. *Growing Yourself Back Up: Understanding Emotional Regression* . Harmony. 2001.

71   **Regarding boundaries:** Anne Katherine. *Boundaries: Where You End and I Begin—How to Recognize and Set Healthy Boundaries.* Parkside Publishers. 1991.

75   **More from Brene Brown on vulnerability:** Brene Brown. *The Power of Vulnerability.* 2010. Retrieved from https://www.ted.com/talks/brene_brown_on_vulnerability?language=en

76   **Would love remain if vulnerability was exposed:** R. Morton, Theron Thomas, Timothy Thomas, Lukasz Gottwald, Henry Walter, Toni Tennile (writers). R City. "Locked Away." R City Feat Adam Levine. *What Dreams are Made Of* [album]. Dr. Luke-Cirkut Producers. Kemosabe-RCA. 2015.

77   **Brown on Shame:** Brene Brown. *The Power of Vulnerability.* 2010. Retrieved from https://www.ted.com/talks/brene_brown_on_vulnerability?language=en

77   **Shame as a 'soul eating' emotion:** Carl Jung. *The fight with the shadow.* Listener, 7(7). 1946.

86   **Step by step communication tools:** Pia Mellody. *Developing Personal Boundaries.* 2013. Retrieved from https://www.youtube.com/watch?v=7bk_SG2QD4E.

88   **Delineating a hierarchy of needs:** Abraham Maslow. *A Theory of Human Motivation.* [Article]. *Psychological Review.* 50(4), Jul 1943. 370-396.

89   **Primary needs different for women and men:** *John Gray. Men are from Mars, Women are from Venus.* Harper Collins. *1992.*

90 **Languages of love:** *Gary D. Chapman. The Five Love Languages: The Secret to Love that Lasts.* Northfield Publishing. 1992. 2015.

91 **Someone trusts you with a friendship:** *Ralph Waldo Emerson. Emerson: Essays and Lectures: Nature: Addresses and Lectures/Essays: First and Second Series/Representative.* Volume compilation, notes and chronology copyright 1983. Literary Classics of The United States, Inc. New York, New York. Penguin Putnam, Inc. 1841.

Part 3: Now Us

92 **Mutually satisfying weirdness as 'true love':** Robert Fughum. *True Love.* Harper Collins. 1997.

93 **Defending the Caveman:** Rob Becker. *Defending the Caveman. One man comedy show.* 1991-2006. 2015. Retrieved from www.youtube.com/watch?v=NSxO0ivq0KI

95 **The space for eroticism:** Esther Perel. *Mating in Captivity*: *Unlocking Erotic Intelligence.* New York, NY: Harper. 2006.

96 **Alone I am a complete circle...** Tuesday Thomson, Editor. 1995.

97 **The search for intimacy:** Osi Mizrahi. 2013. *The Search for Intimacy—'In-to-Me-See'.* Huffington Post. August, 2013.

97 **Psychologist Harriet Lerner's "Dance" metaphor:** Harriet Goldhor Lerner. *The Dance of Anger: A Woman's Guide to Changing the Patterns of Intimate Relationships.* New York: Harper Collins. 1985.

98 **Lerner writes about becoming "de-selfed" and the distancer/pursuer:** Harriet Goldhor Lerner. *The Dance of Intimacy: A Woman's Guide to Courageous Acts of Change in Key Relationships.* New York: Harper Collins. 1989.

98 **Psychologist and leading expert in couples' therapy John Gottman described:** John Gottman. "The Distancer/Pursuer

Pattern." recently *The Seven Principles for Making Marriage Work.* John Gottman and Nan Silver. Harmony Books. 2015.

101 **Weaving together boundary concepts:** Pia Mellody. *Developing Personal Boundaries.* 2013. Retrieved from https://www.youtube.com/watch?v=7bk_SG2QD4E

104 **The Four Agreements and Disagreements:** Don Miguel Ruiz & Janet Mills. *The Four Agreements: A Practical Guide to Personal Freedom.* Amber-Allen Publishing. 1997.

106 **John Gottman, "The Einstein of Love":** Kristin Ohlson. "The Einstein of Love." *Psychology Today.* October, 2015.

109 **Television in the 1950's and 60's:** *Make Room for Daddy*: 1953-57. *The Danny Thomas Show.* Television series. Sheldon Leonard. Desilu Studios. 1957-64.

109 **Father Knows Best:** *Father Knows Best.* Television series. Rodney/Young Production. 1954-63.

109 **Questioning the merits of marriage:** Written by Jacob Brackman & Carly Simon. Carly Simon. *That's the Way I've Always Heard it Should Be.* On *Carly Simon.* Elektra. 1971.

109 **Perfect Mother Anxiety:** Judith Warner. *Perfect Madness: Motherhood in the Age of Anxiety.* Riverhead. 2005.

111 **Connection or isolation:** Gary Turk. *Look Up.* 2014. Retrieved from https://www.youtube.com/watch?v=Z7dLU6fk9QY

112 **The Chip Bowl:** Rob Becker. *Defending the Caveman. One man comedy show.* 1991-2006. Retrieved from www.youtube.com/watch?v=NSxO0ivq0KI

114 **Fifty Shades of Grey:** E.L. James. *Fifty Shades of Grey.* Vintage Books. 2011.

114 **Demonizing Male Sexuality:** Alyssa Royse. '*The Danger in Demonizing Male Sexuality'.* 2013. Retrieved from http://goodmenproject.com/featured-content/the-danger-in-demonizing-male-sexuality/

122 **Psychologist Harville Hendrix**: Harville Hendrix. *Getting the Love You Want: A Guide for Couples.* Henry Holt and Company. 1988 (revised) 2007.

125 **Brene Brown on vulnerability and connection:** Brown, B. The Power of Vulnerability. 2010. Retrieved from https://www.ted.com/talks/brene_brown_on_vulnerability?la nguage=en

126 **Vulnerability in music**: Dan Hill. "Sometimes When We Touch" on *Longer Fuse* [album]. 20th Century Fox Records. 1974.

127 **Loving in the 'now':** Meghan Trainor Featuring John Legend. "Like I'm Gonna Lose You." Written by Meghan Trainor, Justin Weaver, and Caitlyn Smith. On *Title* [album]. Epic Records. 2014.

127 **Tim McGraw on living**: Tim McGraw. "Live Like You Were Dying." On *Live Like You Were Dying* [album]. Written by Tim Nichols & Craig Wiseman. Curb Records. 2004.

127 **What Gottman says makes relationships succeed:** "The Einstein of Love": Kristin Ohlson. *Psychology Today.* 2015.

128 **Osi Mizrahi speaks about intimacy:** Osi Mizrahi. *The Search for Intimacy, 'In-to-me-see'.* 2013. Blog post retrieved from http://www.huffingtonpost.com/osi-mizrahi/the-key-to-intimacy-_b_3822974.html

128 **Prostate cancer survivor on intimacy:** Michael Russer. *"Creating Extraordinary Intimacy in a Shutdown World".* 2015. Retrieved from http://tedxtalks.ted.com/video/Creating-extraordinary-intimacy.

131 **Sex 'is coming out of the closet':** Same sex marriages, Caitlin Jenner on gender conformity. 2015.

131 **Best seller on sex, romance and BDSM:** E.L. James. *Fifty Shades of Grey.* Vintage Books . 2011.

131 **Sticky: A (Self) Love Story:** Nicholas Tana's *Sticky: A (Self) Love Story.* Vision Films. 2014.

133 **"Women's Sexuality Emancipation Proclamation.":** refers to women claiming and keeping their sexuality instead of giving it away.

133 **'Bases' and obligatory sex:** explains how many women give up their sexual identity and shut down.

136 **Women's sexual pain:** frequently not disclosed or understood.

139 **Coming back to your senses:** Sensate focus. William Masters, M.D. & Virginia Johnson. *Human Sexual Response.* William Masters & Virginia Johnson Masters. Bantam Books. 1966. Updated 1986.

142 **Helping women become orgasmic:** Lonnie Barbach. *For yourself: The Fulfillment of Female Sexuality.* Doubleday. 1975.

142 **More information on orgasms**: Julia R. Heiman, Ph.D. and Joseph LoPiccolo, Ph.D. *Becoming Orgasmic: A Sexual and Personal Growth Program for Women.* Prentice Hall. 1976.

143 **Men and sexuality**: Bernie Zilbergeld. *The New Male Sexuality.* Bantam. 1992.

143 **More about men's sexuality:** Michael Bader. *Male Sexuality: Why Women Don't Understand It—And Men Don't Either.* Rowman & Littlefield Publishers. 2008.

144 **Connecting opposite ends of the intimacy spectrum**: *John Gray. Men are from Mars, Women are from Venus.* Harper Collins. *1992.*

144 **When things don't work well in the bedroom**: William Masters, M.D. & Virginia Johnson Masters. *Human Sexual Response.* Bantam Books. 1966. Updated 1986.

147 **Good in Bed—sexual communal strength:** Jennifer Bleyer. *Good in Bed.* Psychology Today. September, 2014.

147 **Men whose wives want to have sex:** *Weeds.* Television series. Lion's Gate Television. Showtime Networks. 2005-2012.

148 **Erotica websites**: Mark Schoen. Sex Smart Films. www.sexsmartfilms.com. Tony Comstock. Comstock Films. www.comstockfilms.com.

149 **The wedding cake sexual metaphor:** Developed by Neil Cannon, Ph.D., and Lisa Thomas, Licensed Marriage & Family Therapist. *Happy Healthy Couples: The Wedding Cake of Sexual Fulfillment.* 2012.

150 **Sexual self-pleasuring:** WebMD. Retrieved from http://www.webmd.com/sex relationships/guide/masturbation-guide

151 **Teaching children about healthy sexuality:** Esther Perel. *Talking to Your Kids about Sex.* Web blog Post. March, 2016. Retrieved from http://www.estherperel.com/blog/

152 **"Sex is a natural function.":** William Masters, M.D. & Virginia Johnson. *Human Sexual Response.* William Masters & Virginia Johnson Masters. Bantam Books. 1966. Updated 1986.

152 **Additional Information regarding self-pleasuring:** WebMD. http://www.webmd.com/sex relationships/guide/masturbation-guide

153 **AASECT**: American Association of Sex Educators, Counselors and Therapists. https://www.aasect.org/

153 **The normalcy of masturbation:** Nicholas Tana. (Producer-Director). *Sticky: A (Self) Love Story.* Motion picture. Vision Films. 2014.

153 **What the Bible says**: The Old Testament. Genesis 38.8-10 (NIV).

154 **Can someone be 'addicted' to porn?:** Was *Playboy Magazine* addictive? The debate continues.

155 **Books on women's sexual fantasies:** Nancy Friday. *My Secret Garden.* Trident. 1973. *Forbidden Flowers.* Pocket. 1975. *Women on Top.* Simon & Schuster. 1991.

157 **A moving news story concerning gender conformity:** Kelly Wallace. CNN. *When Your Young Daughter says, "I'm a boy" Raising Ryland.* 2015. Retrieved from http://www.cnn.com/2015/03/18/living/feat-transgender-child-raising-ryland/

157 **Gender non-conformity movie from the David Ebershoff novel:** Tim Bevan & Eric Fellner, Producers. Tom Hooper, Director. *The Danish Girl.* Focus Features. 2015.

157 **The movie from the Patricia Highsmith novel:** Elizabeth Karlsen, Stephen Woolley & Christine Vachon, Producers. Todd Haynes, Director. *Carol.* Killer Films. 2015.

159 **Child sexual abuse survivors:** Ellen Bass & Laura Davis. *The Courage to Heal: A Guide for Women Survivors of Child Sexual Abuse.* Random House. 2002.

160 **College campus rape in the United States:** Amy Ziering, Producer. Kirby Dick, Writer & Director.). *The Hunting Ground.* Documentary Film. The Weinstein Company. 2015.

161 **From *The Hunting Ground* Documentary:** Lady Gaga. "Til It Happens to You." Lady Gaga & Diane Warren (Songwriters). Digital download. Interscope. 2015.

163 **RESOLVE support group:** The National Infertility Association is a non-profit, charitable organization, who works to improve the lives of women and men living with infertility. http://www.resolve.org/?referrer=https://www.google.com/

164 **Redirected passion for new mothers:** Esther Perel. *The secret to desire in a long-term relationship.* Video file. 2013. Retrieved from https://www.youtube.com/watch?v=sa0RUmGTCYY

165 **Postpartum Depression:** A more severe and longer lasting form of depression occurring to some women after childbirth for which there are support groups and professional help.

167 **"Think in terms of my child, my teacher":** Richard Carlson. *Don't sweat the small stuff with your family: simple ways to*

keep daily responsibilities and household chaos from taking over your life. Hachette Books. 1996.

169 **Beyond Dr. Spock-great news on help for parenting:** Gary Ezzo, M.A. & Robert Bucknam, M.D. *On Becoming.* Parent-Wise Solutions, Inc./Hawksflight & Associates. 1995-2015.

170 **Teaching children about feelings through film:** *Inside Out.* Jonas Rivera, Producer. Pete Docter & Ronnie Del Carmen, Directors. Motion Picture. Walt Disney Pixar Animation Studios. 2015.

171 **1500 days of preadolescence to prepare for the 3700 days of adolescence:** Gary Ezzo, M.A. & Robert Bucknam, M.D. *On Becoming.* Parent-Wise Solutions, Inc./Hawksflight & Associates. 1998-2015.

171 **Twain on his father's ability to learn:** Mark Twain quote.

172 **Laughter is the best medicine:** Stephen Colbert. *I Am America (And So Can You!).* Random House. 2009.

181 **Infidelity occurs even in happy relationships:** *Esther Perel: Rethinking infidelity...a talk for anyone who has ever loved.* March, 2015. Retrieved from
https://www.ted.com/talks/esther_perel_rethinking_infidelity_a_talk_for_anyone_who_has_ever_loved?la

182 **Healing after an affair:** Janis Abrahms Spring, with Michael Spring. *After the Affair: Healing the Pain and Rebuilding Trust When a Partner Has Been Unfaithful Completely Updated Second Edition.* 2013. Harper Collins. First Edition. 1996.

182 **Forgiveness:** Janis Abrahms Spring, with Michael Spring. *How Can I Forgive You: The Courage To Forgive, The Freedom Not To.* Perennial Library/Harper & Row Publishers. 2004.

183 **"To err is human: to forgive, divine.":** Alexander Pope. *"An Essay on Criticism, Part II".* 1711.

183 **Common usage quotes that stand the test of time.** Arnold Stein. *Donne's Harshness and the Elizabethan Tradition. Studies in Philology. 137-38.* 1944.

184 **The freedom not to forgive:** Janis Abrahms Spring, with Michael Spring. *How Can I Forgive You: The Courage To Forgive, The Freedom Not To.* Perennial Library/Harper & Row Publishers. 2004.

184 **Staying in the relationship after the affair:** *Esther Perel: Rethinking infidelity...a talk for anyone who has ever loved.* Video File. March, 2015. Retrieved from https://www.ted.com/talks/esther_perel_rethinking_infidelit y_a_talk_for_anyone_who_has_ever_loved?la

185 **Collaborative Divorce—healing while ending:** Dave Moore. 2010. *Happier Endings Through Collaborative Divorce.* D Magazing Special Edition Legal Directory. 2010.

186 **Not for women only:** Lynette Triere with Richard Peacock. *Learning to Leave: A Woman's Guide.* Contemporary Books. 1985.

186 **Blending families:** Emily B. Visher, Ph.D. and John S. Visher, M.D. *Stepfamilies: Myths and Realities.* Citadel Press. 1979.

190 **Change:** David Bowie. "Changes." *Hunky Dory* [album]. RCA Records. 1971.

191 **Successive approximation:** Changing one step at a time.

192 **Couples as therapeutic agents:** Harville Hendrix. *Getting the love you want: A Guide for Couples.* Henry Holt and Company. 1988. Revised 2007.

192 **"Loving someone deeply gives you courage":** Lao Tzu. W. S. Poland. Courage and morals. *American Imago, 64*(2), 253-259. 2007.

Afterword

194 **Know how much you're worth:** Jessie Belle Rittenhouse. "My Wage". Literary critic, compiler of anthologies and poet. The Little Book of Modern Verse. 1917.

References

AASECT (American Association of Sex Educators, Counselors and Therapists). Retrieved from https://www.aasect.org/

Angelou, M. (1988). Interview in *USA Today*.

Bach, G. R., & Goldberg, H. (1974). *Creative aggression: The art of assertive living.* Wellness Institute, Inc.

Bader, M. (2008). *Male Sexuality: Why women don't understand it— And men don't either.* Rowman & Littlefield Publishers.

Barbach, L. (1975). *For yourself: The fulfillment of female sexuality.* Doubleday.

Bareilles, S., & Antonoff, J. (2013). Brave [Recorded by Sarah Bareilles]. On *The Blessed Unrest* [Digital Download] Epic Records.

Barrie, J. M. (1911). *Peter Pan.* Hodder and Stoughton.

Bass, E., & Davis, L. (1988). *The courage to heal: A guide for women survivors of child sexual abuse.* Random House. (updated 2002).

Becker, R. (1991). Defending the Caveman. [One man comedy show]. (2015, April) [Video file]. Retrieved from www.youtube.com/watch?v=NSxO0ivq0KI

Anonymous Content et al. (Producers). McCarthy, T. (Director & Co-writer). (2015*). Spotlight* [Motion picture]. United States: Open Road Films.

Bevan, T., & Fellner, E. (Producers). Hooper, T. (Director). (2015). *The Danish Girl.* [Motion picture]. Great Britain: Focus Features.

Blavin, A., & Blavin, P. (Producers). Dick, K. (Director). (2015). *The Hunting Ground*. [Documentary motion picture]. United States: Chain Camera Pictures.

Bleyer, J. (2014). *Good in Bed*. Psychology Today.

Bowie, D. (1971). Changes. On *Hunky Dory* [album]. RCA Records.

Brown, B. (2012, March) *Listening to Shame* [Video File]. Retrieved from https://www.ted.com/talks/brene_brown_listening_to_shame?language=en.

Brown, B. (2010, June) *The Power of Vulnerability* [Video File]. Retrieved from https://www.ted.com/talks/brene_brown_on_vulnerability?language=en.

Cannon, N. and Thomas, L. (2012) *Happy Healthy Couples: The Wedding Cake of Sexual Fulfillment*.

Cannon, N. (2015). *Happy Healthy Couples: The Wedding Cake of Sexual Fulfillment*. [Webinar].

Carlson, R. (1998). *Don't Sweat the Small Stuff with Your Family: Simple ways to keep daily responsibilities and household chaos from taking over your life*. Hachette Books.

Chapman, B. N. (1991). Save Yourself [Recorded by Suzy Bogguss]. On *Aces* [Album]. United States: Liberty.

Chapman, G.D. (1992, 2015). *The Five Love Languages: The secret to love that lasts*. Northfield Publishing.

Colbert, S. (2009). *I am America (And so can you!)*. Random House.

Columbus, C. (Producer). Barnathan, M. Green, B. (Producers). Taylor, T. (Writer & Director). 2011. *The Help* [Motion picture]. United States: Touchstone Pictures.

Comstock, T. Comstock Films. Retrieved from http://www.comstockfilms.com.

Cosby, B. (1998-2000). Kids Say the Darndest Things. [Television series]. CBS Production.

Cross Canadian Ragweed. (2002). *Cross Canadian Ragweed.* [Studio Album]. Universal South.

Daquila, G. A., & Emerson, R. W. (2012) *Trust: A Retrospective on its Role in the Leader-Follower Equation.* Retrieved from http://geralddaquila.com/2012/10/17/trust-a-retrospective-of-its-role-in-the-leader-follow-equation/

Del Vecho, P. (Producer). Buck, C. Lee, J. (Directors). (2013). *Frozen* [Motion Picture]. United States: Walt Disney animation Studios.

Dick, K. (Writer & Director). Ziering, A. (Producer). (2015). *The Hunting Ground.* [Documentary Film]. The Weinstein Company.

Echosmith, David, J. Dzwonek, J. (2013). Cool Kids [Recorded by Echosmith]. On *Talking Dreams* [Studio Album]. United States: Warner Brothers

Emerson, R. W. (1841). Essays: First Series. *The Dial.*

Emerson, R.W. (1983). *Essays and Lectures (Nature: Addresses and Lectures/Essays: First and Second Series/Representative Men, English Traits, and The Conduct of Life).* Penguin Putnam, Inc.

Ezzo, G., & Bucknam, R. (1995). *On Becoming Baby Wise: Giving your infant the GIFT of nighttime sleep.* Parent-Wise Solutions, Inc./Hawksflight & Associates

Ezzo, G., & Bucknam, R. (2001). *On Becoming Preteen Wise.* Parent-Wise Solutions, Inc./Hawksflight & Associates.

Faust, B. Golin, S. Rocklin, N. Sugar, M. (Producers). McCarthy, T. (Director). McCarthy, T. (Writer). (2011). *Spotlight.* [Motion Picture]. United States: Open Road Films

Felshuh, N. Grant, A. Harris, C. Levin, A. Harris, S. (2015) Renegades [Recorded by X Ambassadors]. *VHS*: [CD-digital download]. KidinaKorner-Interscope.

Fisch, S. M., Truglio, R. T., & Cole, C. F. (1999). The impact of Sesame Street on preschool children: A review and synthesis of 30 years' research. *Media Psychology*, *1*(2), 165-190.

Forward, S., & Frazier, D. (1997). *Emotional Blackmail: When the people in your life use fear, obligation, and guilt to manipulate you.* Harper Collins Publishers.

Franken, A. as Smalley, S. (1992). *I'm Good Enough, I'm Smart Enough, and Doggone It, People Like Me! Daily Affirmations By Stuart Smalley.* Dell Books.

Friday, N. (1975). *Forbidden flowers.* Pocket.

Friday, N. (1973). *My secret garden.* Trident.

Friday, N. (1991). *Women on top.* Simon and Schuster.

Fulghum, R. (2003). *All I Really Need to Know I Learned in Kindergarten: Reconsidered, revised & expanded with twenty-five new essays.* Random House Digital, Inc.

Fulghum, R. (1997). *True love.* Harper Collins.

Goldstein, K. (1939). *The Organism.* Zone Books.

Gottman, J. M. (2015). Gottman Couple Therapy. *Clinical Handbook of Couple Therapy.*

Gottman, J. M., & Silver, N. (2015). *The Seven Principles for Making Marriage Work.* Harmony Books.

Gray, J. (1992). *Men are from Mars, Women are from Venus.* Harper Collins.

Halbert, J., & Olson, E. (Producers). (Clarkson, K. & Halbert, J. Songwriters). (2012). Catch My Breath. (Recorded by Kelly Clarkson.) On *Greatest Hits—Chapter* 1: [album]. RCA Records. Heiman, J. & LoPiccolo, J. (1976). *Becoming orgasmic: A sexual growth program for women.* Prentice Hall.

Hendrix, H. (1988) *Getting the love you want: A guide for couples.* Henry Holt.

Highsmith, P. (1990) *Carol.* Bloomsbury.

Highsmith, P. (1952). *The Price of Salt.* Coward-McCann

Hill, D. (1974). Sometimes When We Touch. On *Longer Fuse* [album] United States: 20th Century Fox Records.

Hill, D. (1994). *Sometimes When We Touch.* [Video File]. Retrieved from https://www.youtube.com/watch?v=IATz8ZVTALo.

Hoffman, E. (1988). *The right to be human: A biography of Abraham Maslow.* Jeremy P. Tarcher, Inc.

Irving, J. (1978). *The World According to Garp: a novel.* Dutton.

James, E. L. (2011). *Fifty Shades of Grey.* Vintage Books.

Jung, C. G. (1946). The Fight With the Shadow. *Listener, 7*(7).

Karlsen, E., Woolley, S., & Vachon, C. (producers). Haynes, T. (Director). (2015). *Carol.* [Motion picture]. United States: Number 9 Films, Films4 Productions, Killer Films.

Katherine, A. (1991). *Boundaries: Where you end and I begin—How to recognize and set healthy boundaries.* Parkside Publishers.

Lee, J. (2001). *Growing yourself back up: Understanding emotional regression.* Harmony.

Leonard, S. (Producer). (1953-1957). *Make Room for Daddy.* (1957-1963). *The Danny Thomas Show.* [Television series]. Desilu Studios.

Lerner, H. G. (1985). *The Dance of Anger: A Woman's Guide to Changing the Patterns of Intimate Relationships.* New York: Harper Collins.

Lerner, H. G. (1989). *The Dance of Intimacy: A Woman's Guide to Courageous Acts of Change in Key Relationships.* New York: Harper Collins.

Lions Gate Television (Producer). (2005-2012). *Weeds.* [Television series]. California: Showtime Networks.

Loesser, Frank. (1950). Sit Down, You're Rockin' the Boat. From *Guys and dolls.* Book by Burrows, A. & Swerling, J.

Lopez, R., & Anderson-Lopez, K. (2011). Let it Go [Idina Menzel]. *Frozen* [Motion Picture]. (2013).

ManKind Project, Petitjean, P. (2006). The Birth of the Scientific and Cultural History of Mankind Project. *Sixty Years of Sciences at Unesco, (1945-2005).* 85-88.

Maslow, A. H. (1943). A Theory of human motivation. *Psychological Review, 50* (4), Jul 1943, 370-396.

Maslow, A. H. (1962). Lessons from the peak-experiences. *Journal of Humanistic Psychology* 1962 2: 9. Sage.

Maslow, A. H. (1958). Some Basic Propositions of a Growth and Self-Actualization Psychology. [Chapter in *The Maslow Business Reader*. (2000) John Wiley & Sons] 31-53.

Masters, W. H., & Masters, V. J. (1986). *Human sexual response.* Bantam Books.

Mellody, P. (1989). *Breaking Free: A Recovery Handbook for Facing Codependence.* Harper Collins.

Mellody, P. (2013, April) *Developing Personal Boundaries* [Video File] Retrieved from https://www.youtube.com/watch?v=7bk_SG2QD4E.

Mizrahi, O. (2013, October) *The Importance of Loving Your Self.* [Blog post] Retrieved from http://www.huffingtonpost.com/osi-mizrahi/the-importance-of-loving-your-self_b_6196492.html.

Mizrahi, O. (2013, October) *The Search for Intimacy, 'In-to-me-see'* [Blog post] Retrieved from http://www.huffingtonpost.com/osi-mizrahi/the-key-to-intimacy-_b_3822974.html.

Moore, D. (2010). *Happier Endings Through Collaborative Divorce.* D. Magazine.

Morton, R. Thomas, T., Thomas, T., Gottwald, L., Walter, H. (2015). Locked Away [Recorded by R. City Feat. Levine, A.]. On *What Dreams are Made Of* [Album]. United States: Kemosabe-RCA.

Nichols, T., & Wiseman, C. (2004). Live Like You Were Dying [Recorded by McGraw, T.]. On *Live Like You Were Dying* [Studio Album]. United States: Curb Records.

Ohlson, K. (2015, October). The Einstein of Love. *Psychology Today, Time, 143*(12), 22.

Perel, E. (2006). *Mating in captivity: Unlocking erotic intelligence.* New York, NY: Harper.

Perel, E. (2015, March) *Rethinking infidelity...a talk for anyone who has ever loved.* [Video file]. Retrieved from https://www.ted.com/talks/esther_perel_rethinking_infidelit y_a_talk_for_anyone_who_has_ever_loved?la.

Perel, E. (2016, March 4). *Talking to Your Kids about Sex* [Web blog Post]. Retrieved from http://www.estherperel.com/blog/.

Perel, E. (2013, February 14). *The secret to desire in a long-term relationship.* [Video file]. Retrieved from https://www.youtube.com/watch?v=sa0RUmGTCYY

Perry, K. (2013). Roar. On *Prism* [record]. United States: Capitol Records.

Poland, W. S. (2007). Courage and Morals. *American Imago, 64*(2), 253-259. (Lao Tzu quote)

Reddy, Helen (1970) I Am Woman (Helen Reddy). On *I Don't Know How to Love Him* [album]. Capitol Records.

RESOLVE support group. The National Infertility Association. Retrieved from http://www.resolve.org/

Rittenhouse, J. B. (1917). *The Little Book of Modern Verse.* Houghton Mifflin Company.

Rivera, J. (Producer). Docter, P., Del Carmen, R. (Directors). (2015). *Inside Out.* [Motion Picture]. United States: Walt Disney Pixar Animation Studios.

Rodney/Young Production. (1954-1963). *Father Knows Best* [Television series].

Rogers, C. (1961). *On Becoming a Person.* Houghton Mifflin Harcourt Publishing Company.

Rousseau, J. J. (1755). *Second discourse. The discourses and other early political writings.* Cambridge University Press, Cambridge.

Royce, A. (2013, May) *The Danger in Demonizing Male Sexuality.* [posted article] Retrieved from http://goodmenproject.com/featured-content/the-danger-in-demonizing-male-sexuality/.

Ruiz, D. M., & Mills, J. (1997). *The Four Agreements: A practical guide to personal freedom.* Amber-Allen Publishing.

Russer, M. (2015). *Creating Extraordinary Intimacy in a Shutdown World.* [Video File]. Retrieved from http://tedxtalks.ted.com/video/Creating-extraordinary-intimacy.

Schoen, M. Sex Smart Films. Retrieved from http://www.sexsmartfilms.com.

Schreiber, F. R., Vigil, L., & Martínez, S. (1973). *Sybil.* Henry Regnery.

Siegel, D. J. (2014). *Brainstorm: The Power and Purpose of the Teenage Brain.* Penguin Group.

Simon, C. Brackman, J. (1971) That's the Way I've Always Heard it Should Be. On *Carly Simon.* [Album]. United States: Elektra.

Spring, J. A., & Spring, M. (2013). *After the Affair: Healing the Pain and Rebuilding Trust When a Partner Has Been Unfaithful,* 2nd ed. Harper Collins.

Spring, J. A., & Spring, M. (2004). *How Can I Forgive you?: The Courage to Forgive, the Freedom Not To.* Perennial Library/Harper & Row Publishers.

Stein, A. (1944). Donne's Harshness and the Elizabethan Tradition. *Studies in Philology, 41*(3), 390-409.

Stockett, K. (2009). *The Help. New York:* Amy Einhorn Books.

Tana, N. (Producer-Director). (2014). *Sticky A (Self) Love Story* [Motion picture]. United States: Vision Films.

Taylor, T. (Writer & Director). (2011). *The Help.* [Motion picture]. Touchstone Pictures.

Tedder, R. (2013) Counting Stars [Recorded by OneRepublic]. On *Native* [CD Single Digital Download]. Mosley-Interscope.

The Old Testament. (Genesis 38.8-10. NIV).

The Old Testament. (Leviticus 19:18. New International Version).

Trainor, M., Kadish, K., Weaver, J., Smith, C. (Songwriters) (2014). Like I'm Gonna Lose You. [Recorded by Trainor, M. Feat.

Legend, J.]. On *Title*. [Studio Album]. United States: Epic Records.

Triere, L., & Peacock, R. (1985). *Learning to Leave: A woman's guide*. Contemporary Books.

Turk, G. (2014, April) *Look Up*. [Video File] Retrieved from https://www.youtube.com/watch?v=Z7dLU6fk9QY.

Twain, M. *"When I was a boy…"*. Attributed in 1915.

Twain, M., & Tuckey, J. S. (Introduction). (1876). Republished (1980). *The Devil's race-track*. University of California Press.

Visher, E. B., & Visher, J. S. (1979). *Stepfamilies: Myths and realities*. Citadel Press.

Wallace, K. *When Your Young Daughter says, "I'm a boy" Raising Ryland*. (2015) [Video file]. Retrieved from http://www.cnn.com/2015/03/18/living/feat-transgender-child-raising-ryland/

Warner, J. (2005). *Perfect Madness: motherhood in the age of anxiety*. Riverhead.

Warren, D., & Gaga, L. (2015). *Til It Happens To You* [Recorded by Lady Gaga]. [Digital download]. United States: Interscope.

WebMD. Retrieved from http://www.webmd.com/

Winnicott, D. W. *The Maturational Process and the Facilitating Environment*. Hogarth Press, 1965.

X Ambassadors. (2015). *Renegades*. VHS album. KIDinaKORNER— Interscope.

Zilbergeld, B. (1992). *The New Male Sexuality*. Bantam.

Index

Made in the USA
Coppell, TX
14 November 2019

11342031R00141